LIVING IN AN ANIMAL RESCUE

A human's life at Modjeska Ranch Animal Rescue

MODJESKA RANCH RESCUE

By Russell Taylor

ISBN: 978-0-692-58988-5

Book design by Ademir Kalač.

Printed in the United States of America.

First printing edition 2022.

CONTENTS

DEDICATION

To Teresa, without whom there would be nothing to write about.
To Rochelle, Chantal and Nikki, 3 beautiful daughters whose
smiles always melt my heart
To Fallon and Darcy, 2 wonderful Grandchildren

INTRODUCTION

This book is an account of almost twenty years running an animal rescue in Southern California. It is not chronological or comprehensive; it is episodic, and its contents are those episodes that I had the time, energy and motivation to write. Some of them will seem to be written in the present tense, because I wrote them as the events were happening and I decided not to change that. Many great/funny stories are still there at the back of my mind or on scraps of paper but if I waited to write them all, this book would be published posthumously. I wrote the first story in 2002, always meaning to "get down" to fleshing out the book and finally I decided to publish what I have, so this is it.

I must emphasize before you even start reading the stories that the impetus for starting Modjeska Ranch Rescue, and the passion poured into it over all these years is not mine. I have I hope supported, and worked hard with, and at times suffered with, the driving force for the Rescue who was, is, and forever will be my wife, Teresa Jackson (she could never be bothered to do all that name changing stuff when we got married, she is always far too busy)

We have rescued, housed or re-homed over 10,000 animals; I admit we have lost count. Although most are/were dogs, cats and horses, we have also had donkeys, cows, small birds, huge birds, goats, sheep, llamas, pigs, chinchillas, chickens, turkeys, rabbits, guinea pigs, turtles and fish. If it sounds crazy...it is!

Modjeska Canyon

This is the view over Modjeska Canyon from outside our house, which has become Modjeska Ranch Rescue. The canyon is named after Helena Modjeska, a famous 19th century Shakespearean actress from Poland who settled here.

Chapter 1

SURPRISE IN THE BATHROOM

Sometimes we are asked what it is like to "live" at the Rescue. As some of you probably know, the main Modjeska Ranch Rescue facility is our home in Modjeska Canyon, where we have 4 acres and a medium-sized house. The dogs all live with us in the house, not in cages or crates, they are part of the family. Sometimes there might be 15 dogs in the kitchen, or 6 dogs on the couch and often there are 12 dogs in the bedroom when we go to sleep. Many other kinds of animals also call this place home. So let me try to give you an impression of a day. This is the first story I wrote about the Rescue, about a year after we started.

It was early. The California sun was breaking onto my bedroom across Saddleback Mountain, and the coyotes had gone to bed for the day. Shafts of light streaked across my sketch of David Hockney at 20. "Lives of the Great English Poets" lay tattered by the side of my bed. Yesterday's New York Times crossword lay half done, as I can never finish Thursday's. I rolled off the bed and gazed from the balcony out over the Canyon. It was a lovely sunny day and I could just catch a glimpse of the sea and Catalina Island in the distance.

I padded out of the bedroom and down the curved staircase, gripping tightly to the black wrought-iron railing to offset the effects of age, sleep, and the remains of a bottle of good wine from the night before.

Near the bottom of the staircase, my bare foot landed on a step softly, yet also squishily.

I hesitated.

"Oh, poop!" I said. I really used a more colloquially appropriate term but "poop" will suffice for the purposes of this story.

Which way should I go? I hopped to the downstairs bathroom and opened the door, to be surprised by four bouncing one-week-old puppies who had "pooped" all over my new expensive tile floor. They had chewed up the newspaper which I assume had been put down to catch "dog discharge fallout" and they now thought jumping up my bare leg with their puppy razor claws was a cute way to get my attention.

4

I surveyed the scene, smelled the odor, felt the claws, and closed the door in a period of 3 seconds, having had to fend off the persistent advances of the puppies with my feet and hands and try not to slam their heads, paws etc in the rapid closing (slamming) motion.

I had, in the chaos, forgotten the "poop" from the stairs which had still been stuck to my left foot, and which was now spread across the whole of the sole of my foot, and also on the hallway tile and door.

Before I had time to react, swear, or question the origin of the puppies, Teresa called from the kitchen and said, "Careful if you go in the downstairs bathroom; there are puppies in there!" That comment of course robbed me of the chance to make some smart remark about what I'd found in the bathroom, and that is exactly what it was designed to do.

You will remember that I am still stood outside the bathroom, wearing only PJs, with poop on my foot, and scratches up my leg. I am at the far end of the house from the next nearest bathroom. The kitchen, whilst large, is already full with one person, 25 dog bowls, 3 huge bags of dog food, sinks full of bowls needing cleaning, and two pans of boiling chicken and rice for the dog's breakfast.

Where do I go to clean up?

At this point I still do not know the culprit for the "pile" on the stair-carpet, if you will excuse the pun. A DNA test is out of the question, and its size and form have already been rendered useless for evidentiary purposes by the heavy descent of my foot. Suspects are many and a confession is unlikely.

Starting an animal rescue was a decision we took without a specific plan of how large it would get, how long we would continue, and how much of our home and bank account we would dedicate to the animals. I suspect that, had we had such a discussion, agreement would have been difficult to reach. In fact, when people ask me about starting the rescue, I do not say I agreed to it, merely that I acquiesced!!

The strategic creep of the space taken up by the rescue until we lived in it ourselves was imperceptible. One day I woke up and there were animals in my bed, in my bathroom, in all my bathrooms, in my garage, in my kitchen, and in the acre of ground I have carefully landscaped with 10,000 plants.

For a man who loves elegant decor, silence, quality furniture, old books and, above all, the smell of clean things, this would seem like hell on earth.

In truth, there are days when it is just that, or something worse if it exists. The contrast of my ideal lifestyle to the one I live is as jarring as "George Bush sings Aerosmith's greatest hits".

I'll probably get letters now saying George W is a great rock n' roll singer. Maybe he is!

However, there is another truth to this picture, which I cannot fully explain yet myself.

We have created something that is admired by many and has achieved amazing things. We started by just rescuing 2 dogs from a shelter. As of 2022, when I am editing this, we have done over 10,000 adoptions in almost 20 years and care every day for between 20 and 30 dogs, mostly elderly or sick, some cats, goats, horses and pigs and a sheep. We have rescued dogs, cats, sheep, horses, including wild Mustangs, cows, llamas, birds, pigs, goats and even chinchillas.

I like animals. I just hadn't planned to be further down the list of priorities than the ones in my own house, all 40-50 of them!

I do get tremendous satisfaction from successful adoptions of animals which would otherwise have been "dead meat" and caring for old, unwanted animals who just need TLC, medication and a warm, comfortable place to lie down in their "Golden Years", even if that warm place is where I was intending to sit or sleep myself

What is constantly surprising is the enormous need for what we do, and, at the same time, the weird, funny, sad, encouraging, dispiriting and even enraging events that accompany the pursuit of saving animals from death.

This book will tell you some of the happy, sad and funny stories from the past 20 years. I wish I had written them all down, but I was too busy picking up poop.

The Welcoming Committee at Modjeska Ranch

Approaching Modjeska Ranch Rescue can be intimidating for the un-initiated. Would you believe I used to get repeated calls from salesmen insisting I should have an electronic alarm system. I assure you if someone breaks into my house, there's a good chance they won't get out again.

This picture is a favorite of many Rescue supporters, I just wish I had taken a better-quality version of it. As you can see everyone is happy to greet whoever is coming down the pathway. The tableau is usually accompanied by a lot of noise of course as the dogs say "Hello" in their own language. We do not encourage strangers to approach without us being around, but there are some who find their way in and wander up to this scene without fear, which worries us from time to time as some of the dogs are older and cranky and some can be jealous for attention if they are not getting their fair share.

The eagle-eyed will notice that there are seven...count them ....SEVEN Great Danes in the picture. We became known for being willing to take and care for older and sick Great Danes, even from relatively far away. You may wonder why someone 150 miles away would contact us about a dog; are there no Rescues much closer that can help? Well, often the answer is

"No". A Great Dane is often a friendly, relaxed house dog, but they are very big! They take up space and they eat a lot, so that presents challenges that most rescues are not equipped to handle. Add to that most rescues do not have their dogs roaming free like ours and that presents cage/dog-run/space issues to be handled.

The fact that Teresa has always loved Great Danes could have had some influence on which dogs we agreed to intake.

A few of the crew relaxing in the smaller fenced area outside the kitchen. The kitchen door is open, and they can wander into the house and out of the other side to the large, enclosed area if they wish. However, they would all rather be close to wherever we are at the time.

Chapter 2

BUYING A HOUSE

How did we acquire the property that became Modjeska Ranch and start the Rescue?

Modjeska Ranch is not the name of some 10,000-acre Spanish Land Grant Ranch that we have acquired, it's just a name we gave our house when it became the rescue in 2001, and the name seems to have stuck. We do have 4 acres of land, which is unusual in this part of Southern California, but 10,000 acres would have been nice for the horses, goats and dogs. We bought the house in 1999 from a Dutch couple who had built it in 1979. It's sort of back to front, with the back of the house facing the street, which has puzzled me at times, but it may be because the sun pans across the front of the house throughout the day most of the year, hence the sun does not pan across the back of the house where the living room and kitchen remain out of direct sun all day. In the summer we will get a number of 100-degree F (38C) days and many days in the 90s. As the needs of the animals for many years led us to leave the doors open most of the time, this shaded part of the house is at least a few degrees cooler than the Sahara, even if it is not traditional Southern California air-conditioned living. As the doors were always open for the dogs we do not use the antiquated A/C system in the house, which is a 40 year old heat pump with what feels like the power of a children's bicycle.

I am often asked how we found the house, as Modjeska Canyon is still not well known and in 1999 many people even locally had no idea where it was (long may that continue!). I call Modjeska the last hidden paradise in Orange County. I would tell people we were moving to Modjeska Canyon, and they would say "Mo-where ......is that in California?" It is in fact only 2 miles from our old house and very close to the "concrete", but it's still a secret to many. I am amazed by how many people live within a few miles of this beauty but simply have no idea that not only is it beautiful, but the original house of Helena Modjeska is still here, and Tucker Wildlife Sanctuary is here also. Helena Modjeska was a very famous 19th century Shakespearean actress from Poland and her Queen Anne-style house was designed by Stanford White in 1888. It is a National Historic Landmark and can be toured by arrangement with the county. Local enthusiasts even started performing Shakespeare and running a children's summer Shakespeare camp there in 2018, kudos Dion Sorrel who is also an awesome electric cellist.

Back to how we found the house. My Mother was visiting from England for Christmas. I had gone to work. Yes, I had a normal corporate job. I had been President of a well-known franchised service company in UK at the age of 30, set up new operations in the Middle and Far East and then set up a Joint Venture with another multi-national company to bring the operation to the USA. This company insisted that I was part of the deal, so I came to the USA to do acquisitions and form and run an operation here which I did. The personal journey from that to running an animal rescue is a long and very complicated story in itself but not one for today.

Teresa and I, before the Rescue, had been foster parents to many children, a couple of them quite long-term but many short-term or even for a weekend (the Respite program to give other foster parents a weekend break). There are many happy, sad and shocking tales from that fostering experience, but that's yet another story for another day. I think there are some parallels though as one of the things that some foster children and rescued animals have in common is a reluctance to trust their new "family", and with some of their shocking background stories that is totally understandable. It takes time and patience and lots of TLC.

As with the Rescue, I completely concede that the driving force behind that is/was Teresa and her passion and courage to make a difference in life whatever the obstacles, even if the obstacle is me!

One day, Teresa and my mother, Rosemary, drove to Modjeska Canyon to visit friends who also were part of the foster program. They are still friends. On the way out of the canyon, Teresa was driving past a house as a new "For Sale" sign went up. My Mother said "Stop", as she was fascinated by this house, and she and Teresa ended up having coffee with the owners. I received a call at work saying, "You need to come and look at this house!" My reply was "I didn't know we were looking for a house!"

Well, two women and one man......what chance did I have?

When we bought the house on its four rather hilly acres, it was in need of a lot of work, and it still is. The previous owners had bred St Bernard's, and not much updating had been done since it was built in 1979 but it is a very interesting design. It has a high ceiling in the family room with a sort of minstrel's gallery.

My intention had been to enlarge the house, update it, and make the grounds special, even with a golf green. Absolutely none of those plans have come to fruition.

There are a few major reasons for that.

-Firstly lack of money which went rapidly to other things as our focus changed to rescue.

-My income source changed dramatically as I gave up the corporate treadmill.

-A fear, or really a knowledge, that whatever attractive improvements we made to the house would soon be impacted by the inquisitive teeth, claws and fur of the 20 to 40 dogs and cats we had in the house.

On top of this is just the normal reason exhibited by most households... life was too busy to do anything about it. For most of the first couple of years after we started the Rescue, I didn't work, but that was not a viable long-term financial situation as you can imagine. In 2003 I started to work as a Realtor, a pursuit chosen as it gave me the chance to make a living but also flexibility in my work schedule which allowed me to be somewhere for the Rescue at a particular time if that was needed. This has worked out well as about two thirds of my Real Estate clients know me through the Rescue and understand that it is this which helps pay to keep the Rescue going. No real estate deals completed translates to no mortgage payments made which means no Modjeska Ranch Rescue. (I wish I could get more of our rescue supporters to understand that but I am not complaining...well not much!)

So back to the house. Before we started the Rescue, we decided that the house needed new carpet. We chose a mid-blue very expensive carpet following my instinct which has always been "Do it once, do it right! This was probably inherited from my grandfather, a very wise man, who often used the phrase "If a job's worth doing, it's worth doing well". The carpet was lovely. However, once we started the Rescue and had sometimes 30 to 40 dogs in the house, the carpet decision started to look like an expensive mistake. Mid-blue thick pile carpet does not respond well to puppies, old dogs, and their various "deposits" and the crazy digging to see what is under the carpet. It wasn't long before the carpet looked and smelled like a men's bathroom at a low-division football game.

We decided to tile the ground floor. It is still tile and this has stood up well many years later despite much abuse, and lots of bleach. We didn't tile the stairs, as the dogs would slip, so the stair carpet at times does look very tattered. It is my job to vacuum the stairs as Teresa contends that it hurts her back to do that which is a fine excuse! This job is a bit of a pain as the staircase is curved and each step is just a tad too narrow to support a vacuum cleaner head. FYI I hate this job!

17 years of animal rescue makes an "impact" and I choose that word advisedly. As I have said, I love clean lines, modern architecture, book-lined walls, art and sculpture, quiet jazz playing in the background and antiseptic cleanliness. None of this describes life in our house. I guess maybe I get that in the next life? The night we moved into the house, Teresa broke down crying. Our previous house had newly installed granite counters and beautiful new solid hardwood floors throughout. This new house was a wreck. Teresa went to bed, and I proceeded to get on a ladder to scrape acoustic tiles off the ceiling and started painting the kitchen, determined to show her that we had not just made a huge mistake. It was a strange time, but we survived and gradually the house started to take shape.

Teresa had, during 2000, talked about the idea of rescuing animals, and emphasized to me, in her own unique fashion, that we had the ideal place to do it. She is a strong, persuasive woman with a PhD in assertiveness! Self-doubt is not her most often displayed characteristic (it is there but hidden well). Having eventually "agreed" with Teresa that we should do this (as I have said earlier acquiesced is a better word), we got started. Neither of us ever imagined that Modjeska Ranch Rescue would grow and broaden the way it did. Our plan was to take a few dogs from death row at the County shelter and see if we could find them a home. There was no grand plan to save over 10000 animals and have horses, cats, sheep, goats, llamas, cows, birds etc.

I spent a lot of time learning how to set up a 501C3 corporation so we could offer people tax-deductible giving. Thank you NOLO press who had a great book on the subject, it was far too early to rely on the internet for such things. For those of you under 25, a book is a paper thing with pages printed in ink! We set up a bank account which we funded ourselves and even got a credit card with a massive $500 limit; would you believe 21 years later our limit is still $500! Back to the story. My business had an office at the time in Santa Ana. About half a mile away was the Santa Ana shelter, which had a poor reputation mostly because the building was terrible. The dogs were in a basement area and it was a dog Alcatraz. One day we ventured out to start rescuing. We went to Santa Ana shelter and took out 2 dogs. Our neighbors in the canyon, Jim and Diane, run a business called American Horse Products, and every year they had a parking lot Bar B Q for clients. They suggested that we take our adoptable 2 dogs to the Bar B Q. We got a couple of signs made by friends who owned a sign business, bought a little table, and set up at the Bar B Q in the parking lot wondering what would happen. I suppose the thought in our heads was a little like someone who opens a new retail store and then wonders if anyone will actually come in!

Well, we adopted out both dogs, almost much to our own surprise! And it was fun, sort of.

The next week we went and took 3 dogs out of the shelter. We asked a well-known pet supply store in Rancho Santa Margarita if we could stand outside the store with the dogs and they said yes. Well, guess what, all 3 dogs got a new home.

At this time of course we did not have 20-30-40 dogs in our house like we do now, but we did have a 7-year-old daughter at home, and a business to run. I was not a realtor back then and Teresa did not work at the Veterinarian office where she later spent 20 years. We spent almost every weekend for the next few years standing outside initially that pet supplies store and then, after they asked us, a rival well-known pet supply store. Sometimes we would take 5 or 6 dogs to the store, and we became the weekend attraction. People would bring their kids to see us and want to leave their kids with us while they shopped! We also learned that not only are there shelters full of dogs, but there are lots of people wanting to give up their animals, for good, bad and indifferent reasons, a few of those reasons we actually believed but some were just either laughable or truly depressing.

At one time early on we had taken in a German Shepherd and she had her 10 puppies in my office. Now you may all think puppies are cute, and ONE puppy is very cute. However, 10 puppies create chaos and a smell that permeates anything nearby; cleaning up is a full-time job and not one for the faint-hearted, or the well-dressed. They can also challenge the laws of Physics. I was taught "Matter cannot be created or destroyed"; well how come you can feed a dog one pound of food and three pounds seems to come out of the other end! Of course Teresa's recollection of events may be different so maybe that's another story!

It's been a roller coaster ride, with joy and tears mixed in roughly equal amounts, but we are still here

A very early Modjeska Ranch Rescue picture. They are in the backyard just hanging out. A variety of breeds and ages all getting along.

Chapter 3

A CLOUDY DAY AT MODJESKA RANCH RESCUE

The morning routine at the Rescue is for Teresa to get up around 5, and make breakfast for Nikki, who leaves early for school, and then start the dog and cat feeding marathon, clean cat litter boxes etc.

I get up around 5.30 (..ish!) and my job is to feed the horses, goats and pigs and clear up after all the dog's natural bodily functions in the front yard and the back yard and anywhere else it is needed, sometimes in the semi-dark, which can be hazardous to the shoes...and the nose...and the fingers. I should wear gloves for this task, but I don't. I know, you are jealous of such an exciting start to the day! You sit there with your coffee and toast dreaming of my morning doggie cleanup delights, don't deny it!

This morning had an added surprise. I say surprise with my tongue in my cheek because this has happened many times before, but each time it is a surprise, and not a fun one. In the living room are 2 couches, on which the large dogs, Great Danes, St Bernard, Greyhound etc. like to recline in regal splendor by the fireplace which I recently had to rebuild (details later). Well, this morning the room looked like the view from an airplane at 30,000 feet, you know the view of the top of the clouds which is endlessly fascinating, pure white and fluffy. It seems that at least one canine wrecking crew, but I suspect more, had decided to investigate the inside of the couches, obviously convinced that something tasty was deep down there in the cushions and frame stuffing.

The whole room was covered in couch stuffing! Pairs of eyes were staring at me saying "What's the problem?"

As I stand there with a large wad of stuffing in my hand looking at them and saying, "What's this!!" they all look at me as if to say "Well, it's the inside of the couch, isn't it? Stop whining and get us another one!"

Of course, after the first few wrecked couches over the years, we stopped buying new ones. When a couch is destroyed, we make an appeal to Facebook friends or email list readers to give us their old couch when they replace it with new. Of course, the condition of couches we are offered, and that people think it appropriate to offer, varies greatly. Sometimes we get offered great couches that have obviously been changed for reasons of taste and décor, but sometimes we get offered ones that look like they have been

15

thrown off a cliff and then trampled and peed on by horses. In the latter case one can uncharitably wonder occasionally if we are just a convenient way to dispose of heavy trash. Sometimes also the couches smell of animals and of course we cannot really discern that until we have them at the house. You may think "But you are a Rescue, why does that matter?" Well, as you now know all the dogs live in the house and use the couches and often the beds. However, what surprises anyone who visits us for our rare entertaining activities is that our house does not smell of animals, it is very clean and generally a nice place to be, because we work hard to make sure of that, despite the large pack of dogs and other critters. We bleach the floors regularly, clean surfaces with good cleaners and sometimes dilute bleach spray, Lysol spray and Febreze in large quantities. We do not do this for the animals, or for the visitors. We do it for ourselves so we can stay sane. That is not to say the house is always in tiptop condition as there are marks on the walls from dogs, and the kitchen cabinets at knee level show a lot of wear and the windows at knee/waist level have dog-nose marks most of the time no matter how often we clean. However, in general the house is clean and smells OK. Anything lingering is dealt with anyway as Teresa is a lover of smelly candles, especially expensive ones.

I digressed again!

We did make the mistake one year of treating ourselves to a really nice leather sofa and loveseat set; it cost about $3000. Six months later a Mom boxer decided to have her pups on the sofa and it was never quite the same. This was despite the fact that we had set up a custom whelping station for her. The nice brown leather couches were obviously more to her liking.

The Fireplace I mentioned above was a very nice one of dark wood and Dutch tile inlay (there was a time when this was very stylish) It was nice when we bought the house. Earlier this year, the wood was "removed" by some very strong teeth leaving just the 14-inch-high framing, inside which one curious dog got himself completely stuck! How he wriggled in there and turned round so his nose was looking out is a mystery. He looked so forlorn, unable to move and whimpering. We had to saw the frame to remove the dog who then thought it was all great fun! I have since re-covered the whole frame with 16-inch tile. It looks quite nice actually and I know the dogs appreciate my efforts.

Now we have cleaned up the "cloud" and it is time for a quick cup of tea before leaving for work.

No doubt the dogs all want to know when the new couch is coming. Don't hold your breath guys!

These slides are from a Powerpoint presentation we gave to supporters many years ago and give you an idea of the variety of animals over the years.

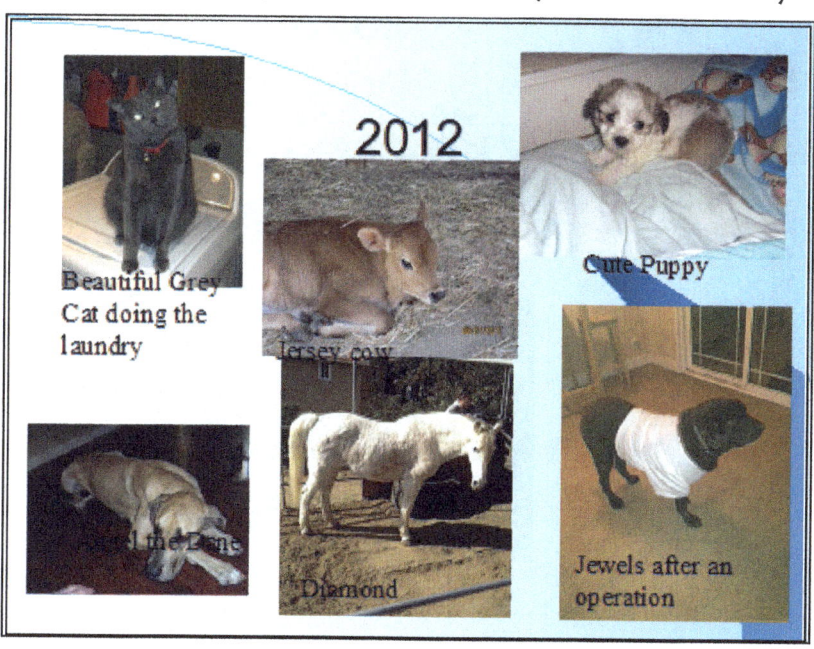

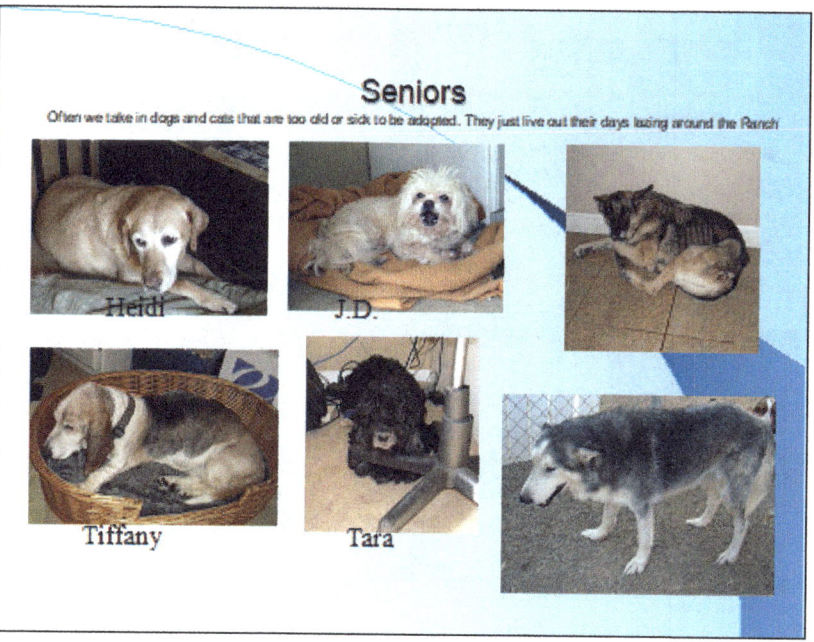

2013

Hannah was hit by a car and brought to us

Chick the "Appendix"

Sam the Labradoodle

Buddy now lives in San Francisco

Harry now has a new home

Buddies

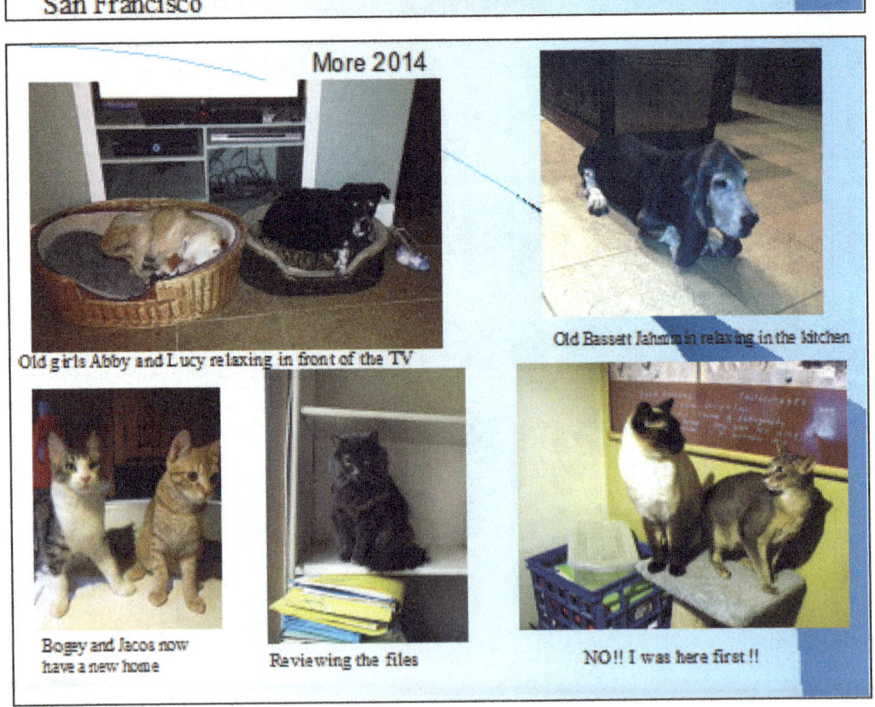

More 2014

Old girls Abby and Lucy relaxing in front of the TV

Old Bassett Jahmm in relaxing in the kitchen

Bogey and Jacos now have a new home

Reviewing the files

NO!! I was here first !!

Chapter 4

BEDTIME AT MODJESKA!!!

Going to bed at Modjeska Ranch Rescue does not simulate "going to bed" anywhere else I can imagine, apart from some amalgam of "Animal Farm" and "Alice in Wonderland". Peaceful it is not; romantic it is not. Remember that, in contrast to many people's visions of an animal rescue, all the dogs and cats live in the house that is the rescue, my house, which I share with my wife and daughter and usually at least 20-30 dogs and some cats and there's been a lamb and a pig and a Moluccan Cockatoo and 2 Blue and Gold Macaws and some finches. I admit that the horses, goats and usually the pigs are outside thankfully.

When it is bedtime, any semblance of logic or comfort for a human is overwhelmed by the needs, desires and peccadilloes of the dogs.

On those occasions when we have a lower "inventory" of dogs, and the rare chance presents itself to have maybe only 4 dogs in the bedroom, Teresa will find some pretext to "invite" more dogs from other parts of the house to join us. It's as if she needs a "quorum" for a meeting. Maybe she just wants enough to keep me far enough away from her! A canine chastity barrier. An understandable feeling some might say but I protest I'm pretty damn sexy for my age.

The rationale presented for having new dogs in the bedroom ranges from "Well this one is new, and I don't want to hear it crying all night" ...to.... "It's a Basset and all it will do is bark" to "It's cold tonight and it's warmer up here". The latter expression of concern is voiced in the context of having the bedroom door open to the patio all night so the dogs can go out, and also, when it is cold, having the electric heater on next to the open door so we can keep the dogs and the whole neighborhood warm whilst also going broke paying the electric bill.

One of the other occasional rituals is that Teresa will suddenly decide, halfway through getting ready for bed, that one of the dogs needs its ears cleaned. I am not sure of the synapse sequence which causes this timing decision, but if you have ever smelled the liquid which is used to clean a dog's ears, you will understand why I am not a great supporter of bedtime ear cleaning, especially if one must observe the results of the ear-cleaning which are presented by Teresa on a disgustingly black earbud as evidence of why it needed to be done right now!

We have a California King bed. What we really need a Worldwide Dictator bed. It's strange, as soon as Teresa gets in bed, the dogs all want to be on the bed. If I am in the bed on my own, they don't get on it. Teresa is comfortable in bed with multiple dogs as she sleeps in one position and has no trouble not moving. She is one of seven children and I think this is part of the explanation. I am an only child. I need to move in bed, shuffle, turn over, stretch my legs out, then move them, then fidget and turn again. The dogs do not understand this and like to lie firmly on my feet! I cannot tell you how much I must love Teresa because I hate anything on my feet, but I tolerate it, most of the time.

On the rare occasions that we go away and stay somewhere nice, we both remark on how nice it is to have a quiet, clean bedroom, with soft bedding, nice smells, and carpet to keep our bare feet warm and cozy. I try to remark that this is how most people live and we could too if we organized our menagerie a little differently, but, as those of you who are married will understand, my argument is met with a reaction which can only be described as impolite disbelief based on the "impossibility" of us ever living with less than 20 dogs in the house.

We have fake wood flooring in the bedroom. It is quite soft and easy to clean but I would not say it was attractive or comforting, and it shows dog hair, of which we accumulate large amounts! I keep threatening to tile the bedroom with something attractive, but the money needed to do that has always already been spent on dog food, cat food, hay, Vet bills, electric bills etc.

There are three other attractions to our bedroom at Modjeska Ranch.

Firstly, in the early days of the rescue we would have food down in the bedroom, in case they were hungry. Well, it seems that settling down to sleep is a signal for at least one dog to decide it's time for dinner. Trying to sleep with an incessant crunching in my ears is impossible. One dog crunching food in an otherwise silent room is loud!

Secondly, for some reason, dogs like to drink out of the toilet bowl, even when there are ample supplies of water in other more appropriate receptacles. Once again, it seems that, switching off the lights is the time at which at least a couple of dogs will patter loudly across the floor into the bathroom and start lapping and slobbering in the toilet! I have almost got used to that, but the really annoying thing is that having been properly brought up by my mother to put the toilet seat down, I climb into bed to hear the grey-hound banging the seat top up and down as he tries to get his head under the seat into the bowl. Now, of course, this is MY FAULT for leaving the seat down, which is so bred into me that it is an unthinking action...I can't change that. So, I start to get out of bed to go and put the seat up but some-times Teresa will say, "No, I'll get it!" in that tone of voice which implies that I am an idiot!

Thirdly, most of the dogs that end up in the bedroom are getting old. Their ability to release noxious gasses in an appropriately open-air setting is gone, and there are nights when one feels that a police tear gas attack would be easier to survive. I swear it really is the dogs.

I think there should be a Rescue budget for 2 nights at the Ritz Carlton every month just to get a good night's sleep and a little sanity. Donations should be sent to....

As I have said earlier, we seemed to become known as the place to call if there was a Dane in need. Here are a few from the archives

Raining Even More Danes

How many Danes can you get on a couch?

Chapter 5

DOGS IN THE HOUSE AND DOG DOORS

3 Danes relax with their bodyguard

This is a typical scene in the kitchen. The matching direction of the gazes probably means someone is preparing food. The fan in the background shows it must be during the summer. Until early 2019, we did not have dog doors big enough for the large dogs, so the doors were always open, rain or shine, hot or cold, wind or calm, enabling the dogs to go out to do the necessary (spoiler alert...there are always some who don't make it outside which is why our house downstairs is all tile and we use a lot of old towels and a lot of bleach!!) In early 2019 a generous donor (thank you Denise) paid for 3 new dog doors. These were matching solid doors with 39 inch dog doors custom fitted for the side door of the house by the fireplace and for the bedroom where a door leads out to a large upstairs patio. Then there was a very expensive custom glass kitchen slider with a 39 inch dog door in the glass. This has made a huge difference to us. We had spent 18 years getting used to being freezing in the winter at night and roasting and sweaty in the summer. As I have said, our A/C system is 40 years old. If we turn it on, it is not very effective. However, being able to close the doors has been a huge boon

26

and we have discovered that our house must be well insulated and decently built as it stays quite warm without heating in the winter. Funny how small things can change your life!

Cozy Bulldogs

There is more than one way to keep warm. Who says the French and the English don't get along? Mooshoo and Pixie the French Bulldogs are on the bed with with Diesel the English Bulldog sharing body heat. Mind you Mooshoo the Frenchie has his butt stuck in Diesel's English face, so maybe that is a subtle message.

More Danes on the Couch

Emily sat on Rambo on the couch

Scooby sat patiently hoping Rambo and Bella will need to go outside soon.
Notice the couches change often as they get torn up.

Chapter 6

ANNIE THE CATTLE DOG

About 2 miles from our house is Williams Canyon. You will miss it from the main road as the entrance looks like a small private driveway, but it winds its way back into the hills with some nice old houses, a few shacks, and lately a couple of huge new Tuscan-style mansions. The latter look a little out of place to me but then everyone to his own.

A house had recently sold at the back of Williams Canyon. The house stands on about an acre with plenty of open space, a large, covered porch and a big driveway that curves around some trees making a sort of huge traffic circle.

Well, the old owners of the house had left behind their dog. They had taken themselves, their cars, their furniture, and their belongings, but not their faithful old friend "Annie". I have never quite "got it" as to why someone would do that, but then I don't understand child abuse and torture either, yet it exists in the crazy pantheon of human existence.

We were asked if we could help with Annie, who had never been on a leash, did not have a collar, and had never been off the property. Annie spent her days wandering around the grounds or sat on the porch.

I drove down there in our black Honda CRV with a large crate in the back and the seats folded down, parked by the little circle of shrubbery in the round driveway, and got out. Annie could see me clearly and was not going to run up and say hello to this stranger. Annie knew something was not right.

Annie was a rather rotund brown, red and white Australian Cattle Dog (Queensland Heeler). I tried to approach Annie, who appeared to have a large growth on her side. Annie evaded the pursuit for about an hour, but eventually we managed to get her into the crate and into the back of the Honda. The growth on her side was huge, literally about half the size of a rugby ball and the same shape which looked very strange. I called the Vet office and took her straight there. Randy the Vet tech helped me get the crate inside (I was not going to take Annie out and risk her getting away). The Vet, Dr K, operated that day to remove the growth and then I collected Annie and took her to Modjeska Ranch to recuperate. I was a little concerned how she would fit in with all the other dogs who live free in our house as Annie had been such a loner.

However, over the ensuing weeks Annie became part of the household, very friendly to humans but not really caring about other animals. She was happy to hang around as she had at her first home, lie down in a shady area and watch the world go by, wouldn't we all like to do that.

Annie lived with us for about 5 years, and we loved her. One evening, Teresa had invited some Veterinarians over for a drink. This was quite unusual as we don't socialize as much as we would like, we are just too busy. Anyway, we were at the bar chatting and I went into the kitchen, then returned quickly to grab Teresa. Annie was not moving, she was in the kitchen on the floor, looking to be asleep, but she was gone. Teresa was inconsolable, she just lay on the floor with her arms around Annie crying her eyes out. Despite having lots of animals through Modjeska Ranch, and most of them becoming loved, there are quite a few that become part of you. Annie had some golden years of TLC at Modjeska and that is what we exist to provide in many cases.

Teresa loved Annie so much she wrote a book just about Annie's story, written in the voice of the dog. It's very good.

Cover of Teresa's book on Annie

Chapter 7

BATHTIME AND THE GREAT DANE WITH A BROKEN LEG

It was Sunday night at Modjeska Ranch. Most people we know seem to have spent the day watching football, having breakfast at the beach, sleeping late, visiting family or just pretending to do chores around the house while cradling a beer (or two). I seem to remember, a long time ago, when lots of coffee, huge Sunday newspapers, too rare visits to church, and maybe a phone call to Mom was the agenda for this "Day of Rest". I get the distinct impression that it's not just my life that has changed over the years, which I can attribute to now being a Realtor and running a sizeable animal rescue, but it is actually a different set of life realities experienced by many; relaxation in California is something almost stolen by the filling of one's time with work and toil, as time not spent being productive is almost frowned upon.

Having been brought up in Europe where a couple of weeks every summer is generally spent on vacation somewhere without work interruptions, the American habit of less vacation time and shorter breaks was a shock to the system. When I came to the US, I insisted that my contract from my multi-national corporate employer included a "normal" 5 weeks of paid vacation. I don't think I could ever take it even though I was the President of the US Company but it looked good on paper.

Anyway, I digress again.

It amazes me occasionally the way some of the dogs that we take in end up arriving on our "plate".

To start with this week, we have taken in a fun black cocker spaniel, allegedly with mange. We are testing her, and she may be OK, but she needed a good bath which we gave her this morning in the sink in our kitchen. I think she enjoyed it! Lots of suds everywhere. Hope our septic tank survives.

Also, this morning several High School students came to volunteer. There are normally a few on the weekends. Some come to do their school-required community service, and a few come just because they want to help.

It's always useful, although it's generally dirty cleanup work which some of the "school-required" volunteers find unpleasant, they would rather just pet the dogs or brush the horses. One volunteer turned up in her Gucci loafers and played with her cellphone while her mother cleaned out horse poop! Another couple of guys turned up to plant new plants on a large area of bare hillside, claiming that they were experienced at it. They spent a day putting little colored flags all over the hillside to indicate what they were going to plant....and never came back.

Later in the morning we took in a larger brown and white cocker; his owner is old and no longer able to care for him. We found that he is lively for an older dog and can climb one of our fences in the smaller dog area, so we are taking a little extra care with him. He seems to be settling down and gets on well with all the other dogs.

Now to the Great Dane story.

Well, the next morning, Teresa was driving to a shelter in Thousand Palms to collect a 1-year-old black Great Dane mix. The dog had a broken leg from a car accident but was said to have a very sweet disposition. We hoped to be able to do something with the leg and then find the dog a home. Of course, in the interim period there was probably going to be an ortho-pedic surgeon's bill. We sometimes get a break (not a pun) on the bill, but nevertheless it's expensive. What amazes me is that a small private rescue such as our own, more than 2 hours' drive away, is the one which gets calls from concerned people, and other rescues, asking us to intervene.

So that next morning...the Great Dane was called Delilah and, as I said, she came to us from a public shelter in the desert. We are quite well known in some rescue circles and attract calls from people who think we can do what nobody else will. One of those niches we seem to fill is with large dogs, especially Great Danes but others also. It is understandable of course. Great Danes are very large, eat a lot and don't live to very old age (although many of ours have made it to 11 or 12 or even older). At one time we had seven Great Danes, all wanting sofa space or even to sit on a lap!

Back to Delilah. By the way, we had decided by this point that she was maybe mixed with Doberman, but still very pretty and just the shiniest pur-est black coat you can imagine, like a soldier's black dress boots. Delilah had been hit by a car and had a badly broken leg. Some people would say "why didn't the shelter fix this?" Well, in my experience the shelters are fighting a battle as best they can but have financial and political challenges that make life very hard. If you don't think your local shelter is doing a good enough job, start with the local politicians who make the policies and the budgets, not the shelter staff who are probably doing their best in difficult circumstances.

We have fixed broken legs before and know a great orthopedic surgeon in Orange County who did agree to help at a reduced fee. Delilah had her leg fixed even though the surgeon said it was very bad and he couldn't guarantee it would work but he would try. It did work because he is a very good surgeon!

While Delilah was recovering at our house, about a week later, she started to become very lethargic. This was a concern. During some further investigation, it turned out she also had a hernia, probably from the same accident that broke her leg, and being on her back for the surgery may not have helped the hernia. By the end of the week, we had an ultrasound done and saw that her organs were pushing up into her chest cavity.

More surgery!

The hernia was fixed, and Delilah began to recover well, to the point that she was a very healthy, happy dog. We found her a home with a family which had 3 other dogs and a pool. Delilah is very spoiled, and we see her often. The two surgeries, even at our reduced rate, were $10,000. At the time we were very short of money ourselves, so we paid for the surgeries on our personal credit cards and made an appeal to see if anyone would help us and reduce our cost. We did get support from some great people and most of the cost was eventually covered by donations.

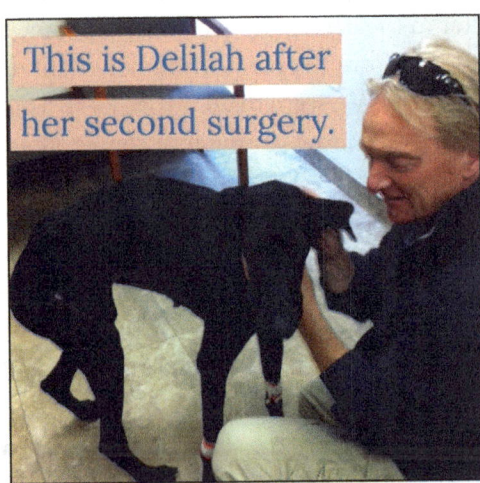

This is Delilah after her second surgery.

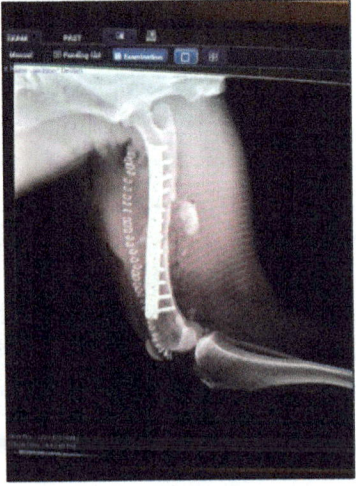

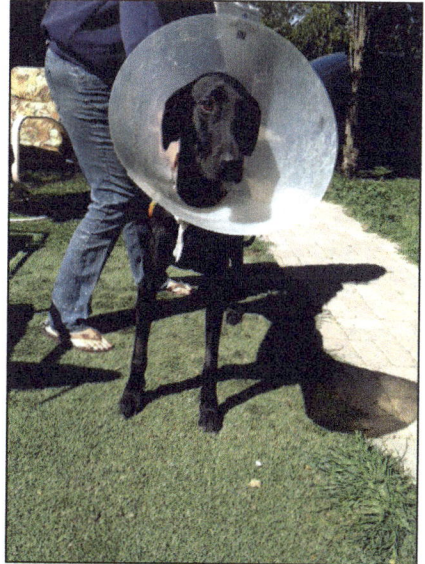 

The bottom right picture is a very healthy Delilah in her new home with her buddy Maggie.

Survival Strategy

By the time evening arrives, I admit that we often end up partaking of a glass of wine and, if you can believe it, occasionally two!

Also, occasionally we do "flee the joint" for an hour on Sunday morning and have breakfast at the Silverado Café, which I heartily recommend. You will not believe you are in Orange County, and the breakfast is such that I don't need to eat for the rest of the day! It is not the best breakfast joint in California though; I reserve that for the Doyle St Café in Emeryville between Oakland and Berkeley. Our youngest daughter was studying up there (I think) and Doyle St Café breakfast is amazing. Try it if you are up there.

Relaxing at Modjeska Ranch Rescue

Brothers Jake and Cody
18 month old Labs

The Three Amigo's

Chapter 8

THE HERO DRIVER

Inside every great endeavor there is a hero...what I like to call a "Hero-Driver". That "Hero-Driver" in Modjeska Ranch Rescue is not me.

A hero driver is selfless - I am far too vain for that. A hero-driver is not tender, a hero-driver is tough, at least on the outside but can be charming when needed. Think Jobs, Musk and leaders who are quite popular and successful but do not court affection.

A hero driver does not suffer fools and does not allow "concept tourists" to waste their time.......the people who want to talk and talk about how they would love to do that if only............or the people who are the "users"...... those who assume that from some tenuous link of circumstance or friendship that they themselves should get special access to benefits or kudos provided by the work of the Rescue rather than just help support the Rescue and the rescuers.

A Hero-Driver is way too busy getting things done to be having meetings about ideas because they already arrived at the idea while everyone else was having coffee and donuts in the breakroom. Everyone just needs to buy into the idea and make it happen. To a hero-driver reaching a consensus means having everyone agree to work very hard to achieve the hero-driver's objectives and not bother the boss with inconvenient details; if there are problems then solve them.

A Hero-Driver makes decisions and get things done......sometimes the wrong things, and sometimes when doing nothing would have been better, but they force change and force progress. You can go with them or separate from them but you can't change them. You can help them and manage the chaos they create so it is more productive and less chaotic but they want change and they won't stop until it's done even if "it" ends up looking nothing like the originally described objective, although they will insist that was their plan all along.

A Hero Driver doesn't care about being liked, only respected (and, ideally, obeyed). They are often not keen on crowds and "pressing flesh" and could be solitary if they didn't need others to do the work.

Many entrepreneurs are Hero Drivers. Their personality enables them to buck the opinion of those that disagree and do it anyway. They are not easy people to be around sometimes, often intolerant, and they can't understand why you just don't "get it" and they won't wait around for you to do so and won't explain it, because it is obvious isn't it? Anyway, it will all be fine if you all just do as you are told!

I used to be President (Managing Director) of a large Franchised/Franchising company and do acquisitions of small companies and set up joint ventures and franchises in a number of countries. An interesting thing about them all was that someone had got them started despite the risk and sometimes because from their point of view it wasn't a risk.

Tangentially, another thing I discovered was that inside every good small business there is a strong woman and if you can't see her, keep looking!

At Modjeska Ranch Rescue, the Hero Driver and the strong woman is the same person. I will let you guess who it is. When we started the rescue, Teresa had discussed it with me, but was quickly really frustrated that we hadn't already got going. It was definitely "Ready, fire, aim". I have written 600-page business plans in the days when five and ten year plans were the "norm". I assure you we started the rescue with about a 600-minute plan, in other words only a plan for what we would do tomorrow and no budget planning at all. I do not recommend it and the fact we survived is amazing. Friends who started other rescues told us stories of going quickly bankrupt but we forged ahead. Ten years later, around 2012, despite or because of having rescued thousands of needy animals, and putting their needs first, we very nearly went broke and lost the house/ranch. Fortunately, we escaped that fate, but there were months of sleepless nights.

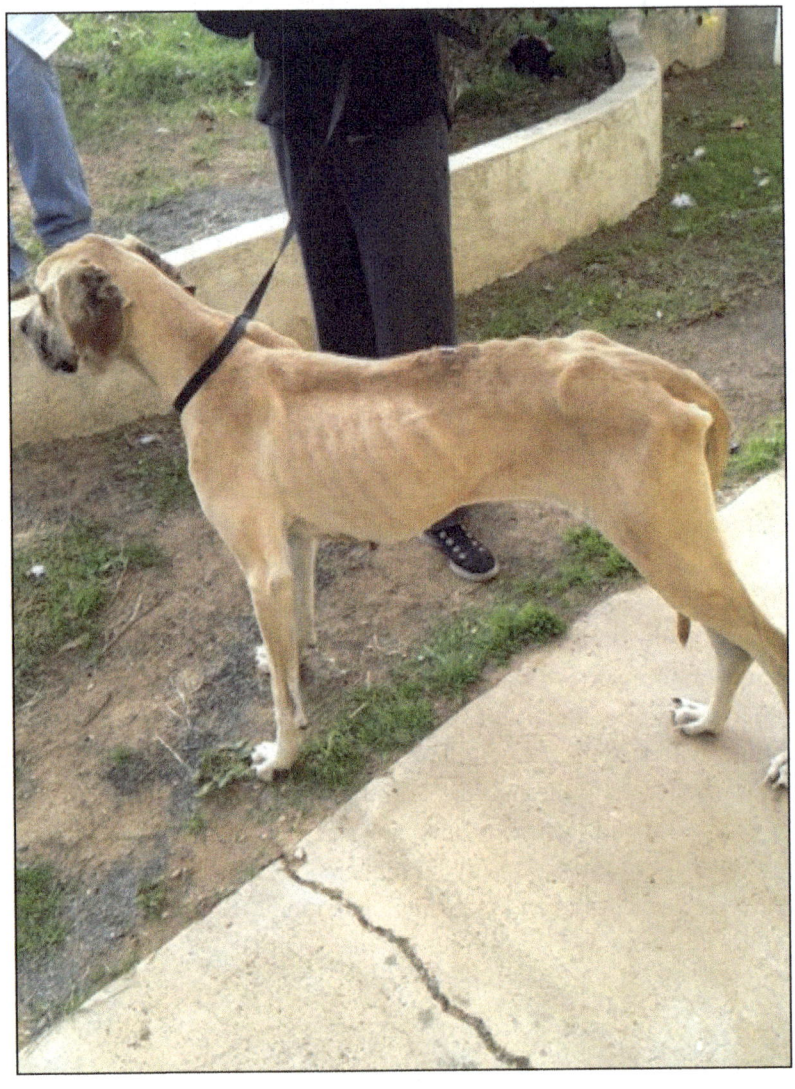

This is Angel, a Great Dane, when she arrived at the rescue, severely emaciated. She put on weight fast and found a new home

Chapter 9

JUST ANOTHER DAY AT MODJESKA RANCH!

Well, it's 8am already. So far today I've fed the horses, goats, llamas and pigs, filled up all their water containers, cleared away trash and talked to them all as if I am Dr. Doolittle. Then I "poop scooped and bagged" each of the dog areas, which is a task and a half when you have as many dogs as we do! The pig's water container then needs to be cleaned out by hand and refilled, every day, for reasons you can imagine but may not want to! If it is cold and raining this is NOT my favorite job! My extra excitement this morning was that one of the goats had found a way out of the corral and was looking at me triumphantly as if he were smarter than me, he probably is as he did not have to clean out the pig's water container!

While I was doing this, Teresa has fed all the dogs, administered pills and TLC to any sick or injured ones, fed and cleaned up the cats, mopped the tile floors which cover our ground floor, fed our daughter her breakfast, emptied and filled the dishwasher (mostly dog bowls), emptied and filled the washing machine (usually full of dog and cat blankets) showered, and left for a work at the Vet office!

Now I get to shower and dress for a day dealing with my clients and the world of Real Estate!

But wait, the phone rings and someone wants to give up a dog. Why would they do that one asks? There is always a reason, some are plausible, and some are, quite frankly, laughable or even despicable. Most people are grateful that we can sometimes offer a way out of a difficult situation, but others treat us like inferior beings and as if we should be grateful to them for "donating" to us such a great dog or cat; sometimes they think we should pay them, as they had to pay so much for the dog in the first place! Some talk to us as if we are the customer service department at Nordstroms or Harrods, telling us what we should or should not do in their circumstance. As you can imagine we normally manage to hold our tongue and not tell them where to stick their attitude, as that would not help the animal.

Meanwhile, back at the Ranch, for a while all is calm. The dogs largely laze around the ranch or play all day. Dottie the deaf white Great Dane, and Randi the greyhound, are asleep on the expensive leather sofa we bought 2 years ago; it lasted barely 12 months as a human sofa before being "annexed" by the dogs. The last straw was when a boxer decided that it was a much better place to give birth to pups than the place we had prepared! We had to buy a new sofa set...I wonder how long this one will last?

Now Lilly the Shepherd has managed to be the final straw on loosening the post attached to the wall which holds one of our wrought-iron gates up inside the house. Have you ever noticed that whichever side of a gate a dog is on, he wants to be on the other side, until he gets there, when he changes his mind! I'll have to get the toolbox out tonight and fix that. I can do it when I am replacing the wires into the back of the computer which have been chewed, again, by a dog who likes to sleep under a desk!

There are usually at least 4 TVs left on in the house all day. The dogs can tell you what you missed on "Days of our Lives" or "Judge Judy". A consequence of that seems to be that we have had to buy 4 new remote controls in the last 6 weeks, as the other ones were chewed to pieces! They must have been bored with that channel.

One or both of us will be back around the house during the day, for the usual routine of filling water bowls, putting in more laundry, and checking on old or sick dogs. Often, I will also have to pick up the remains of books which have been "read" by an intellectual dog. I really, really, love books, even the smell of them, and used to have a lot of them around the house. Bah humbug, who needs books?

As evening approaches, it is feeding, cleaning and medicating time again. It may also involve bringing back a dog or cat that has been to the Vet for treatment or a spay/neuter. Then preparing human dinner, followed by answering as many as 20 phone messages and 20 emails from people regarding the rescue. I would like to say they are all wanting to adopt, but that is unfortunately not the case. More often it is to ask if we will take in another animal, or someone wanting to spend 30 minutes of an already exhausted Teresa's time telling her a story about their animal's hot spot or diarrhea and they don't want to spend money going to the Vet and can she recommend something.

Around 8.30-9pm, we usually check everyone for the night and collapse into bed. There are 7 dogs in the bedroom with us, including a Great Dane, a Labrador, a Retriever, a Boxer, a Greyhound, a St Bernard and a Malti-poo.

Once we turn off the lights, the dogs generally settle down for the night, unless the coyotes start to howl, in which case the dogs respond. The door to the bedroom is open for the dogs to go out which makes for a certain "fresh" feeling when it is raining or cold.

Boomerang the St Bernard and Daisy the Great Dane in the back yard

Chapter 10

CARSON THE GREAT DANE – WHAT A DOG!

(I wrote this in the present tense at the time as an email to our supporters and I decided not to change it)

There are times in life which knot one's stomach with stress and worry. Whatever one's financial position or state of family harmony, or disharmony, events sometimes ambush us and, even for a short time, can drown out everything else going on in our lives. The past few days have been such a time at Modjeska Ranch, especially for Teresa.

I will put this story in context. Many years ago, in the late 1980s, Teresa was living in Ohio, and was "offered" a job transfer/promotion by the large company for which she worked. They even gave her a choice; Los Angeles.......or Anchorage, Alaska (I can hear already how jealous you are)

Teresa's curiosity got the better of her and she did visit Anchorage for a few days to check it out. After that few days the choice seemed to be an

45

obvious one. However, if she'd stayed there I think she'd have given Sarah Palin a run for her money!

Teresa moved from Ohio to Manhattan Beach, about 10 miles south of Santa Monica. Not a bad landing spot I have to say. I wonder if the tanned volleyball players on the beach had anything to do with that choice! The journey from Ohio was made in a 2 door Toyota Celica down Route 66, no doubt accompanied by Chuck Berry or Mick Jagger, and knowing Teresa's driving probably the occasional police car. More to the point she was accompanied by the love of her life, a beige Great Dane called Sheba. Teresa and Sheba used to run together every day from Manhattan Beach about 8 miles down towards Redondo Beach. An idyllic California setting and the perfect relationship as Sheba would do anything Teresa asked (just like me of course).

Sheba lived to be eleven years old, quite old for a Dane, and was always Teresa's buddy. They were "attached at the hip" and Teresa was devastated when Sheba died around 1992, no doubt an emotion many of you pet lovers can understand only too well. It even happened when Teresa was out of town.

Well, fast forward 15 years, and Modjeska Ranch Rescue took in a pregnant blue/grey Great Dane. Three pups were born, two of them blue/grey and one beige, with grey and white markings on his face. He was very cute, and of course there was no way Teresa was going to adopt out this guy to anyone! His name is Carson, after Carson Palmer, who was at the time Quarterback for Teresa's beloved, but usually awful, Cincinnati Bengals. Palmer was also from a place very local to us and went to Santa Margarita Catholic High School.

Carson, the dog, has grown into an almost 200lb beautiful Dane, who is a big lovable baby like most Danes, with big doleful eyes. Visitors to the Rescue think he looks like a small horse!

Well, back to the original story. Last week, Carson became very ill. He has spent a few days at the Vet office on fluids and medication and is now at the Rescue on medications. Part of the problem is that he has trouble eating so is losing weight and although I think he wants to eat, his condition makes that difficult and painful. There are two or three things wrong, and we have to fix them one by one. It is touch and go as I write and, although the medication is being given regularly, it is not certain he will pull through. We must get up early and the medication process takes about an hour for a variety of reasons. Bribery with such things as chicken and peanut butter help a little but it's still a struggle. He just turns away, which is most unusu-al for him where food is concerned. Then we have to try and get him to eat a normal meal to get some strength into him but he's not eating enough.

This whole process is of course not new to us as we have many sick dogs and have had over the years.

We have had successes, and a few painful, upsetting failures in trying to nurse them back to health. Every animal here gets lots of TLC and becomes part of the family......but occasionally one becomes more than that.

I love Carson, he's a big lovable baby, but to Teresa Carson is something more than a lovable dog, he's a direct descendant of Sheba and a link to part of her life.

Of course, the daily routine of the Rescue goes on, as does working for a living.

Many of you support what we do here. Spare a little extra prayer tonight for Carson and Teresa. I am sure many of you have been there and know the torment she is going through.

Postscript: Carson died shortly after writing this, and again while Teresa was out of town visiting family. Carson's condition had declined, and he developed pneu-monia. I spoke to Teresa on the phone, and we decided it was only fair on Carson to let him go. I took him to the Vet office at which Teresa worked and where they were expecting him and knew him. I held him while they did the injection, and he was in my arms as he faded away. I just lay on the floor with him for a few minutes, bawling my eyes out. We miss him.

Carson 2008

Carson with Russell 2012

The White Boxer here, named Brooklyn, was diabetic. As you probably know, insulin for people is very expensive in the USA. I'm tempted to go on a political rant about that, but I will resist. Insulin for animals is also ridiculously expensive. Eventually we found a new home for Brooklyn with someone who was prepared to take on the diabetes situation and give him daily injections, lots of TLC and a fun life. He was always very active, like many boxers, but very affectionate also.

We have had lots of German Shepherds and Belgian Malinois. This sometimes creates a funny scene. Some of the dogs, especially the Labradors like to chase a ball and bring it back for you to throw again. The Shepherds seem more likely to get the ball and then protect it as a prized possession. If there are Labs and Shepherds, this causes some confusion which is amusing to watch.

Lacey is a mini-horse, which means in theory she does not grow more than 29 inches at the shoulder. Lacey and Paco, the black one in the background, are the mini-horses to which I refer in Chapter 15 about the Nun. Paco is a friendly old boy, around 25 years old in this picture, and Lacey is a couple of years younger. Lacey is, shall we say, "less friendly" than Paco, I could use stronger language to describe her moodiness, but we will leave it at less friendly. She always seems to be in a bad mood, I'm sure Paco wonders why he married her, but then he's not alone in the world on that thought, I'm sure. When we decided to get a mini-horse, we arranged it with someone in Arizona, but the horse, singular you notice, had to be collected from there, about 7 hours' drive away. A couple of friends of ours offered to drive to Arizona with a trailer. Of course, no good deed goes unpunished. When our friends reached the farm to collect Paco, the owner stated that we had to take Lacey as well, as they were a pair. Fortunately, the trailer was large enough.

Chapter 11

A SINK AND A SOFA

Every business and family have its disasters. If nobody gets hurt, they are often very funny, in hindsight of course, after the cursing.

As you can imagine, having rescued more than 10000 homeless or unwanted animals and either adopted them out to new homes or given them a long-term home for their golden years at Modjeska Ranch Animal Rescue, there have been times when not everything went quite to plan!

Firstly, remember that all the dogs at the Rescue live at our house, in fact IN our house, not caged or crated, or in dog runs, but in the house, with us, like a huge canine family. Forget your mental image of an animal shelter with lines of dog-runs, think more of a house with a huge family, many of which happen to be animals. Sometimes there are more than 30 dogs of all breeds from St. Bernard's and Great Danes to Poodles and Pomeranians. The cats have their own space of course, separate from the dogs as we just don't know whether new dog intakes like cats as friends or as an appetizer.

Today was a day when my wife, Teresa, was scheduled to do the school carpool pickup run. Well, after receiving a desperate call for help, she instead ended up at a shelter in Los Angeles, about sixty miles away, picking up a sick and rather emaciated St Bernard, and then getting stuck on the great I5 parking lot. For those of you not familiar with Los Angeles, the I5 is the main north-south Freeway from Mexico all the way up to Canada. It is always crowded and frequently backed-up. If you are British imagine the M25 at 5pm on a Friday.

I did the school pickup. No great problem there. A car full of teenage girls discussing issues about which I had no clue at all and insisting that "Mom always stops and gets us something to eat!"

Hold that thought.

Some weeks ago, we took in a female Boxer who turned out to be pregnant. She is a sweet dog and a good mother. She has however, been very expensive!

(For those of you thinking what a lovely way to spend time...saving animals.... "Oh, I would love to do that". Our knowing smiles hide an unsaid response; "No you wouldn't, you wouldn't last a week!")

As our pretty Boxer was nearing the time to give birth, we kept her separate from most of the other dogs at the rescue, cutting off the living room with baby gates. (Will someone please invent a dog-proof baby gate and one that is tall enough for large dogs. Have baby gate designers ever had a dog?)

I arrived home a couple of weeks ago to find her giving birth on our new antique leather sofa to which we had treated ourselves a few months earlier! I have talked elsewhere about learning that we simply cannot buy nice furniture unless we wish to be penniless. She had 8 pups, of which 7 survived. It was a lot of mess and a lot of cleaning, but the sofa was never the same. We could not sit on it without imagining new puppies and the accompanying fluids which go with the marvel of birth.

We have recovered from that. Not too sure about the sofa!

Now back to today!

We had made our downstairs bathroom into a Boxer baby room where Mom Boxer could look after her pups, and we could be close by. Of course, many rolls of toilet paper were sacrificed in this process.

I went to do the school pickup today, and Mom Boxer is fine with her pups, all curled up on a soft dog-bed, calmly feeding her brood. 30 other dogs are happily hanging around in other parts of the house, all of which have access outside to large open areas with views of the canyon in which we live on just over 4 acres.

I got back about 40 minutes after I left and the living room was flooded with 2 inches of water, which seemed to be coming from the bathroom! I opened the door, and Mom must have decided it was time to go out again. She had torn our expensive Kohler Patriot pedestal sink off the wall, smashing the pedestal, leaving holes in the wall and both faucets were on full! I am sure the falling sink had scared her, as the poopy results of her fear were also in ample evidence mixed with all the water! I leave you to imagine that sight. What a mess, and where do you tread?

Fortunately, all the pups were fine, if a little wet. 2 hours of cleaning fixed the bathroom, but we have no sink in there right now. Mom Boxer is fine also and seems to wonder what all the fuss was about.

There were times in my life when I would have been angry, but I had to laugh. I hope my bank manager shares my sense of humor! New sink and plumbing needed. Maybe we make do with a cheap sink.

Emily

This morning, while doing my "rounds", Emily the St Bernard almost leapt into my arms. She does this most mornings, as well as stands across me in front wherever I try to walk. She wants TLC. The remarkable thing is that she came to us because the shelter she was at said she had scoliosis of the spine. She does walk a little like one of those cars that are lower at the front than at the back. Anyway, she leaps around a lot...all 140lbs of her. It's tough to get on with my work cleaning up with a St Bernard trying to sit on my knee.

Here is a picture of Emily with Great Dane Dottie on the famous leather couch I have written about elsewhere.

Chapter 12

FATHER'S DAY AT MODJESKA

Father's Day. A day of rest, often accompanied by a lazy morning breakfast, effusive expressions of affection, presents of books you have already read and ties or socks you won't wear, followed later in the day maybe by a Barbeque in the bosom of the family lubricated with your favorite alcoholic beverage and no comments about whether you shouldn't have another. Altogether, for Dad's generally, a thoroughly nice day when your children forgo the more "age-appropriate" things they would rather be doing and hang with Dad.

OK, so I am exaggerating/stereotyping for the sake of a smile, and my own children are generally fun to be around most of the year and make the effort to humor me on more than one day a year; they are quite convincing in their expressions of appreciation of my "Dad" efforts, so I will choose to believe them.

My Father's Day this year had a little different flavor. One of my daughters, Chantal, decided that she would move house on Father's Day. I have moved her five times before for a variety of college and job-related reasons, even to or from places such as Tempe, Arizona and Delray Beach, Florida.

So, at 7am on Father's Day Sunday I was driving a rental truck, picked up on Saturday night, down to Laguna Niguel where Chantal had rented a storage unit as this was going to be a two-stage move. We had chosen a 10-foot U-Haul and I was convinced it would be plenty big enough because she said many of the pieces of furniture had already been moved. I had not accounted for there being a King bed mattress involved! Much to my surprise the mattress was too tall/long/wide/whatever to stand up in the van. My cousin Craig had come down for the weekend from L.A. , where he worked for Sony Pictures, and had been dragged into this process....poor guy. Maybe that's why he now still works for Sony Pictures but in Vancouver Canada!

Anyway, we did eventually manage to get the bed into the truck, along with most of the other boxes, but we would have been short of space had we not had my youngest daughter Nikki's Honda Pilot with us, which proved to be just what we needed for the extra stuff. Big relief!

We arrived at the storage in Mission Viejo when they opened at 10am. While they were very helpful and pleasant, it always amazes me with these places, as it does with many car-rental places, that even if you have booked in advance, they have 30 minutes of paperwork and questions for you before you can get on with the job! Very frustrating. It should take 2 minutes! "Here is my reservation...give me the key". Why does it take any more than that!! I rent cars in UK whenever I go to see my mom. I have learned to book it in the US through AAA, and insist I get the insurance sorted out and pay for it before I leave as if I don't, I get a 30-minute interrogation when I get to the desk in a UK airport, mostly focused on getting me to pay more money. They once wanted to charge me $50 a DAY insurance because I forgot to arrange it before I left the USA, when the whole car and insurance package would have cost me $350 for 10 days rental including insurance. BTW I took that UK rental car back the next say and told them to stuff it. My cousin Scott picked me up and I managed without a car. (Thanks Scott)

Back to the story. Having gone through the ridiculous check-in at the storage place, we found our unit was on the 2nd floor! (to those of you in the UK that means the first floor...very confusing I know). There was an elevator that was too small for the job. Carrying a large sofa or a King size bed into an elevator and around corners is not an easy task and not good for the cause of inner peace and friendly language.

Anyway, with many trips up and down the tiny elevator we managed to get everything into the storage, but only by stacking high and it was full to the ceiling with many things simply jammed into corners.

Isn't that what Dads are for?

Postscript: Chantal is now married and lives in New Jersey, so I am not the first call for such jobs hopefully.

BULLDOGS

This is Doogie, one of a pair of English Bulldogs we had for a few years. Her buddy Gus you can see in the background. They were a lot of fun with great personality.

We took in quite a few Bulldogs around that time

This is Gus using Mooshoo the Frenchie as a pillow

Gus and Doogie liked to reserve a table for dinner

You always fall asleep when we are in bed together

Chapter 13

GOATS AND DONKEYS AND POODLES-DANGEROUS FRIENDS

Another bright sunny day in California dawned and urged me to awake from my slumbers. I glanced over to the other side of the bed and saw that Teresa was already up, probably downstairs feeding and/or medicating dogs and cats according to their needs. The angle of the sun suggested it was around 5.30am indicating that, in Teresa's mind, I am a lazy lay-about wasting the day in bed when there is work to be done.

I jumped out of bed, landing a fraction of an inch in front of a sleeping Standard Poodle's head. "Chipper" is old, with a shaggy mop of a haircut and questionable eyesight. The startled dog awoke groggily and took a bite out of the back of my leg! It was my fault for not looking where I was stepping, but nevertheless I was quickly reminded that such an experience is painful, and that dripping blood is warm, especially one's own.

Chipper looked at me wagging his tail, "Hey, I'm awake, you can pet me now, and you might want to cut my fringe!"

"Hmmmm...I might just cut your fringe with a machete, Chipper!"

Soon afterwards, blood suitably cleaned up and my leg looking like that of an alligator wrestler, I went up to the corral to do the morning feeding of the horses, goats and donkeys.

The little black goat with straight very pointed horns had found a way out. He is friendly but this morning did not want to go back. He reared up as if to butt me with his horns, so I kept my distance. He ran up and down beside the corral and eventually found his way back in as he saw me putting food in there. I still did not see where exactly he had got out.

Mandy the donkey is not too well right now, so is on some medication. The routine is that I put this in with some "sweet-feed" and hand feed her from a small bucket. That may sound simple, but there are 2 horses, another donkey and 4 goats in the same corral, all of whom like sweet-feed and don't understand why Mandy gets preferential treatment! I am jostled and pushed, and I feel like I am in the middle of a football game with huge linemen trying to tackle me.

After all of this, it is pig feeding time. As I have said previously, Emily the St Bernard likes attention, so on my walk to the pigs, she constantly walks in front of me, stopping all the time so we collide. I have to pet her while walking and push her to make any progress.

What fun!

Now my own breakfast of dry cereal, toast and tea and then to work to make a living so we can pay all the bills and feed everyone. I'm sure they are all supportive of my work as a realtor. Maybe I should parade them around neighborhoods to drum up business for me?

Do you have any multi-grain; it's much healthier!

Goats have a reputation for eating anything at all. It is a well-deserved reputation. For some reason they really love bread, so anytime we have those last few slices of bread in the bag, the goats get a treat. I like grainy bread and sourdough. The goats do not seem to be fussy.

Chapter 14

IT NEVER RAINS IN SOUTHERN CALIFORNIA

Well today it rained. The Medieval saying was "Raining cats and dogs" when it was raining really heavily and today it did. There is more rain to come later in the week and this makes life at Modjeska Ranch Rescue absolute hell.

Today I had gone to work very early indeed, as I was trying to save a client's house from foreclosure during the 2008 recession. The bank in question is on the east coast, 3 hours ahead of us in California. Having spent 3 hours explaining to the bank that this was the fourth time in two weeks they had asked me to fax over the paperwork, and that their protestations that they had not received it were just lies as I did have fax confirmation receipts for each occasion, and I had sent them everything for which they had asked, and had obtained a price they had previously confirmed to me as acceptable, but they were going to foreclose anyway with no explanation! This happened a lot during the recession, when bald-faced lies were often mixed in with total chaos and inefficiency. I was not starting the day in good humor. It seems that logic was not part of bank lending vocabulary and straight answers to straight questions were thought either unnecessary or even legally dangerous. The insane aspect of this is that the lender will be worse off than if they had processed the offer.

Anyway, as you can imagine, by the time I headed home in the early afternoon to meet an adopter picking up Susie the Dachshund, I was a somewhat frustrated person having been unable to save my client's house despite offering the bank everything they had requested.

The adopters for Susie finally arrived, having driven from Redondo Beach, 50 miles, in the rain. All went well, as I dashed out in the rain with Susie under my arm and paperwork in my pocket. To avoid the rain, we completed the formalities in their car, feeling a bit like we were conducting some illegal transaction involving stolen goods or drugs in a deserted rest-stop.

As soon as they left the heavens opened and rain bounced off the ground. The steep street outside our house looked like a river. The hill down from the horse corral to the house looked like a red river, as we stand on pure red clay. I had never seen so much water here. I checked the horses and they seemed fine, despite cracks of thunder and flashes of lightning.

The house and the dogs were not doing as well.

When you spend your property maintenance money on dog food, then I suppose I should not have been surprised when such a rain produced roof leaks in my office, over the bar in the family room, in the bedroom and in my daughter's bathroom. In addition, the big square drain we had installed outside the dog door in the large dog area was blocked with mud and leaves so water was across half the living room inside, which fortunately is ceramic tile. The rain was so hard that, when I was outside, it just went straight though my expensive hiking-style hooded coat, and through my heavy tan-colored work-boots. However, once you are really wet, you can't get any wetter, so you just get on with it. I cleared the drain while being pounded with rain, put tarps on the patio roof, and mopped up inside the house.

Then I went up to the horses. One corral is covered and did well; however, the other one was only erected for temporary purposes originally and does not have side cover, only a roof. The previous day volunteers had put up tarpaulin sides, which were a great idea, but the wind was so strong, it simply ripped the tarps away from their rings. I raked the water and created channels for it to escape but it did seem like trying to push the iceberg away from the Titanic with a broom-handle!

I had left the dogs all in the house. They don't like the rain at all. So, there were a lot of dogs in the house. Most were just doing what they do, lying down and wondering what all the fuss was about. A couple were obviously nervous. The eight Dachshund puppies seemed to think it was great fun.

That could not be said for "Sarah". During the worst of the rainstorm, the mail carrier had stopped at the house and said she had seen a medium sized dog up the road injured, and thought it was a Shepherd. I quickly checked and saw that our brown shepherd was in the house and waiting to be petted, as she is really "needy". I grabbed a leash and intended to go up the road to see what was happening with this dog. Then a car stopped outside, and people from the canyon said they had just picked up this injured Rhodesian Ridgeback and was he ours. I said he couldn't be as our Ridgeback was upstairs right now safely in our bedroom to ride out the storm as we knew she gets nervous, but that friends in the canyon have one almost identical. I said I would look at her anyway. She was wet with an injured front left leg. She looked very familiar and was very friendly, but, as I said, there is one in the canyon that is a "dead ringer" and I was convinced that "Sarah" was upstairs. I said, "Let me just check to make absolutely sure".

Sarah is a "jumper" and we are careful where she goes. She is very sweet but loves to jump out which is why she was brought to us in the first place. Well, the thunder and lightning had scared her so much, she had chewed the bedroom door handle to pieces, cleared the 4-foot railings on the second story patio outside the bedroom and plunged to the ground, and then headed off up the road!

We got her inside and I wrapped her in towels and called Teresa who was working at the Vet office that day. We swapped duties and I headed to pick up our daughter Nikki from school while Teresa headed back to get Sarah and take her to the Vet. Sarah is now back home, with her leg wrapped up, and lying on our bed as if nothing has happened.

So now I just have to find a way to fix the roof and the ceilings, weather-proof the dog doors, and fit a new dog door at the front so we don't always have to leave the door open. Oh, and then work on some side protection for the second corral, which I have already discussed with the volunteers who did the tarp. Oh, and fix the big hole in the stucco where a dog dug his way out of the laundry room a while ago. Oh, and replace the side laundry-room door which now has slipped glass in it and a big hole open to the world.

It is fun running a rescue......really.......no really......honest....why don't you believe me?

Chapter 15

THE NUN STORY

On occasions we are asked to do things to help people. Our usual first thought is that our main purpose is to do things to help animals when people have been the problem! We are sometimes treated like a public service to make other people's lives easier, and our outlook on that is not a very warm and fuzzy one. However, sometimes we do have a situation that touches our hearts, and we respond.

A friend of ours is a nurse and was working at a Hospice for retired Nuns. One of the Nuns was 94 years old and was expected to live only another few months. Her last wish was to stroke a horse.

So, how do you get a horse into a hospital, or even into the grounds. Many people do not realize the real size of a horse. We all see horses on television and in pictures, but not many of us stand by one, look up and think "Wow". An average horse also weighs in at around a thousand pounds or more, so how do you take a horse to a hospital and keep people safe as the horse could get spooked and dance around.

A neighbor suggested that she had a friend with a mini-horse who often takes it to places in the back of her truck, and by that she meant in the back seat space, not the truck-bed. A mini-horse is a maximum of 29 inches at the shoulder, so much easier to handle than a full size animal.

We agreed with the horse's owner to meet her at the hospital. The three of us and a beautiful white, friendly mini-horse walked around the back of the hospital to find 2 large groups of patients, nurses, Doctors and others all waiting for us. The groups, we found out later, were one of reasonably mobile and cognizant patients outside a large door, and then outside a sort of patio garden door, a second group that are suffering from memory loss.

The horse was a big hit, surrounded by first one group and then the other as we moved back and forth in the glorious sunshine surrounded by bushes and flowers. The memory loss group often forgot that they had seen the horse only minutes before and kept asking when they could see the horse. It would be funny if it wasn't so sad.

The big event was still to come.

Everyone stood back, and a nurse rolled out the Nun who was the reason for the visit. She was in a wheelchair. When she saw the horse, her face lit up like a thousand suns and everyone cheered. It was definitely a lump in the throat moment for us all.

We stayed for maybe an hour and it felt really good, so good in fact that we got ourselves a couple of mini-horses from Arizona with the intention of doing things like this again. I have to say that we never did do this again. Why? We both must work full-time to make a living PLUS run the Rescue, caring for usually between 40 and 60 animals every day, with normally just the two of us doing that. We often "run on fumes", up at 5am and fall into bed around 9pm, 7 days a week. We just didn't have the bandwidth to add something to the agenda. We had the mini-horses for many years and they were popular whenever we had visitors at the rescue, but we didn't take them to outside events. It was a good idea at the time but sometimes you have to know your limits.

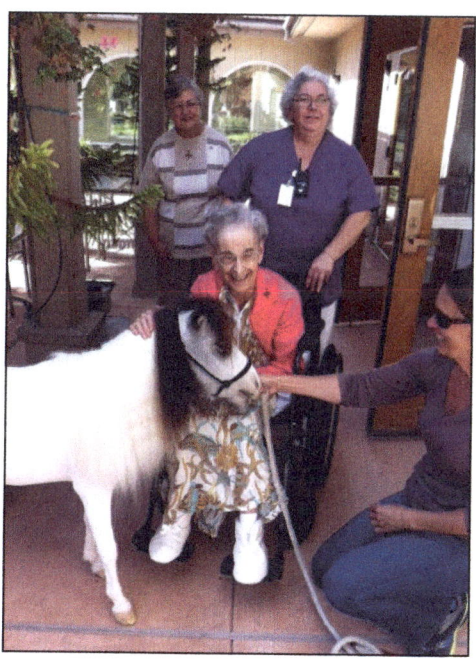

Surfer

Surfer is a beautiful 10-year-old Haflinger horse. He has a lovely temperament. So why is he at a Rescue?

Surfer is blind in one eye and has a club foot but gets around just fine. He may look a little ungainly because when he trots it looks like has a heavy limp, but he seems happy. Surfer's owners had left him behind at a rental property. The property owner called the Horse Vet and asked the Vet to put him down. The Vet refused to do that, and a Good Samaritan called us to see if we would take him. As you can see we said yes.

During the first fire in 2020 we had to evacuate everyone, and Surfer was taken in a horse trailer we thought to Orange County Fairgrounds, but actually the people involved in large animal evacuation took him to San Juan Capistrano about 20 miles south. In San Juan was a family with a large pasture which had been empty since the passing of their horse. As you can imagine there is a certain amount of chaos surrounding even well-organized fire evacuation, so finding that Surfer was somewhere different was not a big problem. The family loved Surfer, and he was leaping around like a young foal and having fun. We had dreams that they might keep him as he looked so happy. Unfortunately, the family had plans that make keeping Surfer impractical, so Surfer came back to Modjeska after about four months away.

Some of our neighbors were happy as they missed seeing Surfer's good looks as they drive by and we have also been asked to lend him to an equine festival for a while where he will get lots of attention, which he will love.

Will you floss my teeth please?

Hannah and Pixie
on the lookout
for strangers !

Hannah and Pixie look very alert. Someone could be coming down the driveway which always causes a commotion, although since there is a Christmas tree in the picture maybe they are waiting for Santa.

Visitors coming down the driveway are a common sight at Modjeska Ranch Rescue. Many bring nice things for us such as old towels and blankets which we can always use, and sometimes dog or cat food, which helps stretch the food budget, as at times we go through 500lbs of dog food a week, about 30 lbs of chicken breast, 10lbs of rice, lots of cat food, and at times when we have lots of horses, we might go through 6 bales of hay. When we had the Mustangs, it was more like 15 bales a week of Orchard hay at $34/bale.

If I am working in my office, the dogs are often very good and just hang around, sleep and play quietly. However, most times as soon as someone comes down the driveway, or even if a car drives by and slows down, the dogs want to let me know, and maybe 15 dogs will begin to bark. Now and again though, I go outside later, and someone has been to drop off donations, and the dogs must have decided to sleep through it and not let me know. The most frustrating time is when I get up, go outside and there is NOTHING. I of course look at all the dogs and say "What? There's nothing, nobody is here!!!!" They all look at me as if to say, "We saw something, we saw something, a white car drove by and it looked like Mom". I go back to work and there are days when they settle down, and then there are days where they seem to see that white car every 15 minutes. My language on those occasions is less than charitable and not suitable for any lady's ears.

Life between meals is so boring

Pedro and Polly the pig just chillin'

Polly came to us as a three-month-old pig. She was bought by someone as a house-pig. The problem was that they lived in a condo complex which of course has rules and regulations, and do not allow pigs. They were told to get rid of the pig "pronto".

Polly still lives in our house, and is not only house-trained, using the dog door, but only poops and pees in one corner of the yard, I wish we could train the dogs to do that.

This picture is Polly chilling with a very old Retriever called Pedro. She may be chilling with Pedro, or she may be trying to nudge him off the bed!

Chapter 16

THE GREAT ESCAPE

Monday morning started eventfully today. Having completed the morning feeding and cleaning regime, I was getting dressed for work and to take Nikki, our daughter, to the orthodontist!

I glanced out of the window and saw Rusty, the 30 something year old horse, out of the corral and strolling towards the street! I ran downstairs, shouting rather intemperate words, and emerged outside to see also that the feisty Shetland Pony, Spirit, who is hard to catch at any time, and the two donkeys, Dandy and Mandy were with Rusty heading for the street!

I was still shouting for help, from anyone, as I grabbed some ropes and tried to form a strategy for one person to catch 4 animals!

Fortunately, some neighbors and a passing canyon friend plus daughter Nikki all arrived to assist.

40 minutes of puffing and panting ensued while scrabbling around the undulating 16 acres behind our house. Business shoes and khaki pants are not well suited to such an endeavor.

Eventually we were successful, but I have to say it was a good way to get the blood circulating early in the morning! The animals seemed to have fun. I have a different word for it!

Later that evening, after I had secured the loose gate with ropes and decided that it was too late to fix it properly that day, I was about to go to bed when Teresa asked me if the goats were out.

It was pitch black so, flashlight in hand, I made my way up the hill to the corral to find one goat looking at me wondering why I was so shiny! He was stood outside the gate that he had managed to force open just enough to squeeze through. He wasn't going anywhere, just looking at me as if to say "Are you going to let me back in then?"

I let him in the other gate and went off, in the dark, to find the right sized wrench to fix the corral gate. There are no lights in my toolshed, so it was not an easy task. My tools are, of course, organized in the fashion of everything in buckets and boxes with no common theme or system!

I found three wrenches which looked about right and headed back to the corral.

They were not the right size. I said to the animals something like "Oh dear, I appear to have the wrong sized wrench. How silly of me" I don't think they were my exact words, but they had similar meaning.

One more trip and I had the right wrench! Hurrah!

As I was on my knees, flashlight in my mouth, tightening nuts on the gate, Rusty the 17-hand horse was leaning over nibbling at my hair. He is always hungry, and I don't know whether he wanted to eat my hair or he was just giving me a heavy hint!

The gate is now secure, and I was able to go to bed without further incident, apart from having to ask a Great Dane, a Rhodesian Ridgeback, a Greyhound and 2 Dachshunds to move over on the bed so I could get in.

Rusty telling me he enjoyed his walkabout

Mandy and Dandy the donkeys

Chapter 17

THE RESCUE, DONATIONS AND TAXES

Modjeska Ranch Rescue is what is called a 501c3 public benefit corporation. This enables people in the USA to donate to the rescue and in most cases make a deduction from their taxes. When we started the rescue, I was constantly surprised how many of the potential adopters of our animals assumed, or sometimes insisted, that we must be supported by the County or the Government, so were offended if we asked for a pittance of a donation when they adopted an animal. We used to ask for $95, which did not even cover the spay/neuter, never mind food, medication, transport etc. Often this was for a young healthy dog which would have cost them $1,000 at the breeder but asking $95 for a dog that has already had all its shots, had been "fixed" and medically checked over, was offensive! We had to bite our own tongues often so as not to be offensive in return.

Some other people just assumed we are rich; our Rescue is based at/in our house which sits on 4 acres in Orange County, California, and that kind of land in this area is unusual and expensive. However, many of you will know the huge difference between being a rich landowner and being someone with a huge mortgage and a monthly heart-stopping payment to make.

There are of course public animal shelters, some very good, some less so, but the need for animal rescue and "re-homing" far outstrips the capacity of public shelters, so private rescues and shelters probably care for more animals overall than the public ones, and these private shelters, like our own, need money from somewhere.

Having said all that, most of our adopters understand and appreciate what we do, and many became friends and cheerleaders for us over the years.

One of the many differences I have noticed as a "Brit" living in America is that, to whatever political or religious persuasion they may adhere, Americans are very generous. Giving money to causes is just part of the fabric of US society. We do not get nearly as much as I think many people assume, but some people have been very generous over the years and some give every month, maybe only $5 or $20, but it all helps. At the year end, before the tax cut-off date we sometimes get an unexpected $500 or $1,000.

We have three or four donors who, over the years, have saved us from being in real financial trouble and we can never express how grateful we are. During the big 2006-2012 recession, my business was dead and donations to the rescue were almost non-existent, yet we had more animals than ever to support as many people were giving them up because dogs, cats, horses etc cost money. As I have said elsewhere, at one point we were so broke that we were three months behind on the mortgage, owed $35,000 on credit cards and Teresa and I lived on those pizzas you can buy at the big box stores, 5 for $5. We would eat a $1 pizza for dinner, but the animals still got fed and cared for.

We were three months behind on the mortgage, had no money, had $35,000 in credit card debt and were eating warmed up pizza every day. I didn't sleep well for a long time. We were only saved by a rescue supporter family who lent us money to pay two months mortgage, and then later refused to let us pay it back. *(Sadly, one of them passed away 2 days before I am writing this. RIP and thank you DW and RW, we can never thank you enough.)*

Rescue is not for the faint of heart and it's not about hugging cute furry creatures. There are moments that change your life and those friends helping us out changed ours. We fought back from that difficult situation, got out of debt, and 5 years later had an 800-credit score. It was not easy, but we remind ourselves now and again how far we have come from those dark days.

Back to taxes. Even though Modjeska Ranch Rescue is a non-profit corporation and doesn't have to pay taxes, we do still have to do a tax return for it. That may sound weird to some, but it has to be done so the IRS can see how much money we raise and what we do with it. I suppose that's reasonable. The only drawback of course is that someone has to prepare the tax return and I learned many years ago that it should not be me. So we have a very good accountant who is well-versed in charity returns. They do a great job.

Chapter 18

THE FENCE AND THE LIVING ROOM

Another day at Modjeska Ranch Rescue. Bruised Hands and paint in my hair

We have some areas of the rescue separated by gates and fences. With cats and dogs of various sizes, temperaments and lengths of residence, we find it important to be able to "divide and conquer". The animals in each area may change week to week or even day to day depending on the comings and goings, but the actual decision as to who goes where is a sort of "Zen" art. There is more intuition in the mix than scientific analysis. After 15 years doing this, that intuition becomes something that we see as obvious common sense, but I am sure someone new to the "zoo" would find such decisions impossible and terrifying.

The fence and gate set-up is an evolving thing. What seems right at the moment may need "tweaking" a little later, or evidence may arise that the way we did something was just stupid in the first place! As with many endeavors, there is a lot of logical planning, a lot of research, and then a lot of trial and error. Anyone who has run any organization, as both Teresa and I have, and tells you otherwise is a big fat liar.

I remember well "Plan your work and work your plan". I think management anywhere is more "Plan your work, work your plan, discover the weaknesses and correct them, repeat ad nauseam"

One of our good decisions early this year was to learn from a couple of good Rescue supporters who told us about some attractive wrought-iron fencing that is easy to install as it fits into stakes that you bang into the ground, rather than having to mess with concrete bases and bolts and foundations. We installed a small section of this fencing in the yard outside the kitchen, so that some of the smaller animals in the kitchen/living room could go out there to hang out and perform their "needs". I should preface this by telling you we have a large, fenced area at the back of the house that is always accessible to the dogs, but our house is built "back to front". The kitchen is by the street, so the new fenced area is to prevent the dogs from wandering away off the premises. Many dogs hang around the kitchen and now they can go out on that side of the house also.

It took about 6 hours to install the fence, mainly because the ground here is solid clay and very hard, in fact in the summer it is like rock. I am told the clay we are on is so pure you could make adobe bricks out of it. Still, the result was excellent.

Of course, no good deed goes unpunished. Teresa decided that she liked this fenced area so much.........that we should make it bigger! She said "just buy 4 more pieces to move each side out another 6 feet, and then move out the whole end section of the fence"

"Easy for you to say" I thought. That word "just" is very misleading. The job did of course not only involve adding 4 more stakes on the two end sections, it involved removing ALL the stakes from the long end and then inserting them again into the very solid clay but six feet farther out. This involved extracting six posts/stakes, then pounding in ten.

The extraction process did not go well. After much shouting and pain, I managed to extract two! Yes, I could have pickaxed each stake but we did not want to do that and leave big holes in the yard, so I went and bought extra stakes and just left a few of the old ones in the ground. It took about four hours, one banged thumb, two blisters on my hands and one totally ruined rubber mallet to finally "just move the fence out another 6 feet". It was about 95 degrees while I was doing this so my normally smiling demeanor was not on view.

The fenced area is now, I have to say, much better. If the Rescue had any money, then next time I would pay someone to do it!

At the same time as I was doing this, I have been painting the living room with the fireplace, which is where a lot of the big dogs hang out as they have a side door to a large run area. I was given an old professional paint sprayer and decided to try it out. It is great but it helps to emphasize the first rule of painting, preparation is everything. Part of preparation is to wear the right "gear". When paint spraying a ceiling, wear a hat! I know I am no longer 20 but any white in my hair I prefer to be natural and not Behr Paint and Prime. Not only did I paint the room and me, but also the hallway and floor and even part of the staircase got the overspray. Now I know why you see those hanging sheets of plastic when contractors paint, because you cannot control the spray to a local area. We still have paint specks on the stair carpet five years later.

Shamu and Bed Destruction

This is Shamu. Some of you will know that Shamu was the name of a large Orca (Killer Whale) at San Diego Zoo. Shamu the Great Dane is a big boy. He likes to play but he sometimes doesn't know his own strength, so the older, small dogs are kept separate from him unless we are around.

He also gets bored. A sofa that has served very well for weeks must suddenly annoy him and he will drag cushions out into the yard and destroy them. I have seen him trying to pull a huge cushion through a dog door which is hilarious to watch so can this is funny, but it is amazing how often this happens when I am short of time, in the middle of something else, or just already very tired. You may think I should just leave it and get to the clean up later. The problem with that is the destruction will only get worse. The filling of cushions and sofas varies a great deal. Pray you never have to clean up destroyed down-filled cushions as it is almost impossible with feathers floating around as you approach. Some foam filled cushions stay in large easy to grab pieces, but many are filled with tiny pieces of foam often of various colors. It is a mess. A broom may do the job, but if the filling is spread out on artificial turf, and wet, then settle in for a long job, maybe with a leaf rake, but I have been known to shuffle around on my knees picking up each piece by hand as it was the only method that worked. You can imagine that my mood at these times is less than charitable.

Sofa Redistribution

Well, my bed just exploded. Have you got another one? What is a Zebra anyway? This was Jade the Great Dane's favorite bed, but it just exploded in her mouth. Strange!!!

Dog beds come in many shapes and sizes. If you have one dog, or two, it seems dog beds can last quite a while. We seem to go through them like paper kitchen roll. With so many dogs, and a constant arrival of new furry friends, there tends not to be a particular bed for a particular dog, they like to change their hotel room often. Also, we have a lot of large dogs and sometimes they get bored. Jade, the Great Dane above, must have got bored this day. The same kind of destruction happens with toys, which are donated to us often, excitedly greeted by the dogs, and torn to pieces quite quickly, which complicates my morning duty of shoveling up the poop, because it has foam and toy bits and bed bits mixed in with it. This is not every day of course, there are days when they are well-behaved all day, but if you have animals or children you know this cannot be relied on to be repeated the next day.

Scooby and Hannah enjoyed tearing this dog bed to pieces, but I didn't enjoy clearing it up.

If I tore up my bed, I would have nowhere to sleep, but our dogs assume, correctly, that we will clean up the mess and give them a new one.

Chapter 19

FUN IN THE RAIN

Fun in the rain!

We are in Southern California. It rains 5 to 10 days a year. To all my old friends in Britain....booooya!

However, about half of those rainy days are real downpours sometimes causing mudslides and debris flows, especially if there has recently been a fire to clear the vegetation. We are on a hill so do not get flooded but we are on clay, so percolation is very slow. It can stay very wet for a few days, and 25 dogs tramping wet, muddy paws into the house and smelling of wet fur is messy and malodorous, but what can we do. The house downstairs is all ceramic tile so we can clean up, hence one use for all those old towels and blankets for which we regularly appeal.

One would imagine the dogs would not want to go out in the rain. That is true of most of the wise old dogs who lay by the fire on a rug and sleep through the wet day, although some of the oldest ones even forget to go outside to pee, hence another reason for all those towels and lots of bleach. We do work hard to keep the place clean and smelling fresh, but it's a job like painting the Golden Gate Bridge; it's never finished.

However, when you have young Labradors or Shepherds, they like to run and chase balls. This picture is Cody and Jake, 18-month-old Labs, who will chase a slobbery ball in the mud all day, don't understand why you are reluctant to pick it up, and then they run into the house and jump on furniture and dog beds with muddy feet and jump up on me or Teresa and run outside again and slide through puddles of mud.

Just Jolly Fun!! As you can see, they also like to drag blankets and toys outside and investigate what's inside the toys or even what's inside a nice foam comforter.

By the way, there is a very good reason why people used to say, "Raining cats and dogs". Medieval houses had thatched roofs (roofs of woven straw). Cats and dogs would routinely jump up there to sleep at night as the thick thatch was a warm place to go. However, when it rained, the straw became very slippery. This led to the people in the house seeing the cats and dogs sliding off the roof when it rained!

This is Jake and Cody without all the mud. They arrived at the Rescue at 18 months old when one of their elderly owners passed away and the remaining owner could not cope with their huge energy levels. They would chase a ball all day and were wonderful but exhausting. We found a great home for them, together, where they are loved and exercised a lot.

<u>Dog City</u>

Sometimes settling down for the evening on the sofa can be a challenge

Gus and Doogie wondering whether to eat the plant or knock it off the table

Chapter 20

FUNDRAISING

We have adopted out over 10,000 animals over 20 years and cared for a lot more which just lived out their days here. The finance of everything is a challenge. Food, medication, Vet care, fencing, corral building and repair, house repair, heating, cooling, beds, blankets, cleaning etc. the list goes on. We have a large online following and are very grateful for all the support we get. However, it is often the same few people who support us financially all the time or bring us supplies and old blankets and towels. I am sure most charities have this issue, so we are not unique. Each year there are a few more regular donors but not nearly as many as you may think. Most people applaud and tell us what a wonderful job we do. Many of them will probably support other charities and we understand there are so many that one cannot support all the ones for which you have an affinity. I do understand that I assure you, but it's a constant struggle to keep the doors open, the animals fed, the Vets paid, the house half-repaired.

We also get "Oh, I would love to do what you do if I had the (fill in the blanks, money, time)". The truth of course is that it is work and more work and a tie on your life; you can't just go away for the weekend, or take a trip to Rome, as someone must look after the ranch. I am not complaining about this at all, merely pointing out that running a Rescue like ours, in our home, with no staff, places restrictions on one's life and finances and one must be prepared for that. After 20 years we are starting to think about how we transition to a semi-retired life with more freedom while we are still young and healthy enough to enjoy it. We will still take in seniors as that is what we do, but maybe not so many.

I suppose that is why so many charities have paid staff doing fundraising. We don't do that. We have only a few fundraising events, Covid and rain willing, as they are very time-consuming and stressful, and both Teresa and I work full-time as well as running the Rescue. The time needed to plan and organize and run fundraising events loses out to feeding, medicating, cleaning etc. One or two people have at times taken on the job of organizing and running events for us, you know who you are, and we are forever grateful for it and apologize if sometimes we are too exhausted to show enough appreciation or occasionally turn down the chance because we just don't have enough energy to do it or have health or stress issues at the time.

Fundraisers have their own interesting and amusing stories when we do have them.

The first Fundraiser we organized was a Christmas dinner at an Italian Restaurant in 2001. We got 70 people to attend, had a silent auction, and a very enjoyable evening. I think we "netted" about $1000 after the costs of putting it on, and 3 months' work to make it happen, which was disappointing, but we felt we had at least learned a lot. A week later we had a call from friends and supporters who had attended and had been multiple charged by the restaurant for their alcohol to the tune of hundreds of dollars. The big mistake the restaurant made was that these supporters were police officers!

Some years later, Greg, a neighbor in the Canyon, suggested he organize an Art Show and wine tasting to support the Rescue. This ended up being an annual event for 7 years and was very popular. We had live music, a great jazz guitarist Joe Baldino, an electric cellist, Dion Sorrel, and for a couple of them we had a Rod Stewart impersonator who was so good some people thought it was him. Each year about 20 artists came with paintings, sculptures, photographs etc for sale and the Rescue got a cut of the sale. It was an amazing event driven by Greg's enthusiasm.

Not far from the Rescue is a famous bar, Cook's Corner. It is a biker hangout and live music venue. Rhonda, the amazing lady who manages it, is an animal lover and like family to us. Each year for a few years there has been a Chili Cook-off competition where Chili cooks from far and wide would come and spend the day cooking all sorts of chili, from scorching hot, to green chili, to veggie chili etc. Visitors would pay for a pack of small cups, and then try the chili and vote on the best one. Proceeds from the sale of cups go to Modjeska Ranch Rescue. It is a fun day. The huge advantage to Teresa and I is that we do not need to organize it or be involved in any way at all except to turn up with a table, an "easy-up" and lots of animal pictures. We would just sit/stand there all day, say hello to people, drink beer and eat chili. Perfect!

I do admit that one reason we perhaps do not have more people involved in fundraising is that we have always valued some privacy and want to control the agenda. The Rescue is our home, and we have at times felt that we needed to have some boundaries. As we both work and run the Rescue, our reserves of energy must be carefully managed, we are no longer 30 years old.

As I write this, we are a year into "Covid". No fundraising gatherings are possible of course. We are thankful to those who donate anyway, sending us checks, dropping off animal food, beds, blankets and towels. We try to thank everyone who helps, we send out thank you cards or emails whenever we can, although sometimes there is "stuff" in our driveway and we have no idea where it is from, so if you left something...THANK YOU.

This is an example of the printed newsletters we used to physically mail out before the days of Mailchimp emails.

M O D J E S K A   R A N C H   R E S C U E

GETPET@aol.com

It's been a busy year again at the Rescue and we have not updated you as often as usual. Hope you like these pictures of some of the recent residents of the Rescue. Jack the poodle mix sat on the sofa below needs a home. I just managed to catch a rare event below where these dogs in the kitchen decided to sleep in a row like a parking lot! The kitchen shot on the right is breakfast time.

Kasey top left is a friendly old Dane. Cooper the Dane on the right came to us with a large growth on his leg. You can see it wrapped on the picture. We have had the growth removed and he is fine. If you have a home for a pretty cat, look at the bottom left. Princess the shepherd is adoptable. You can see a typical living room scene below right. As you know all the dogs get to roam about the house and doors are always open for them to go outside (unless it rains!). No room for the horses and goats on this page.

You can donate online at www.ModjeskaRanch.com

Chapter 21

THE MODJESKA NIGHT-TIME SCREAMER!

I have a screamer in my bed! Sleeping in my bed at Modjeska Ranch Rescue for any extended period at the moment is a feat of considerable difficulty. I have, over time, become reluctantly acclimatized to the presence of 3 to 7 dogs on the bed and maybe a few more on the floor, so that is not the challenge.

We have a member of the Rescue household named MooShoo. He is a rather overweight French Bulldog. Mooshoo likes to sleep on the bed, but only for short periods of time. He will get on, and get off, and get on, and get off etc.

This would not be so bad if it wasn't for the manner of his mounting and dismounting, if you will forgive the expression. For those of you unfamiliar with Frenchies, they do not usually bark like most dogs. I have heard it described as beginning in a low growl and ending in a high pitch shriek. If you were not looking at him, you would think someone was strangling him. It is very loud and disturbing. It would not be out of place in a horror movie.

When Mooshoo wants to get on the bed, which is usually just as I am trying to fall asleep, he will come round to the side of the bed just by my head, and begin to shriek, and shriek, and shriek!!

He will ONLY get on the bed in that spot by my head, which is no lower than any other point on the bed, such as by Teresa's head, or at the bottom of the bed, but it has to be by MY head.

Then he acts as if he can't get up on his own! He shrieks until I pull back the comforter to reduce the height of the bed by at least half an inch and pat the bed repeatedly saying, "Come on Mooshoo, get up". After a shriek or two (sometimes from me) he just leaps up on to the bed, tramples right over me to Teresa's side of the bed and settles down. 20 minutes later he will get down again. Then an hour later, he is shrieking by my head as if he has been abandoned in a sewer by his cruel carers.

Perhaps if I speak to him in French he will understand; "Silence!, s'il vous plait. Tais-toi!"

This does not seem to disturb the other dogs at all. They just sleep through it. I will have to find out how they do that.

Of course, such a night of slumber prepares me perfectly for an early morning cleaning up dog poop, and feeding horses, goats and pigs etc.

Mooshoo

Mooshoo the Frenchie with Bailey, an old English Bulldog.

Gus and Diesel on guard

Chapter 22

CHICK THE QUARTER HORSE

(written present tense when sent out as an email to supporters)

We have just taken in a new horse, a rather elegant brown girl who is mostly Quarter-Horse, I believe the term is she is an "Appendix". Her name is Chick, which sounds a little non-PC for Orange County! I don't think I could get away with calling a young lady "Chick" these days!

The usual routine is that the horses, which number three right now, are fed by me in the morning and get alfalfa plus some alfalfa pellets, and a treat of some "senior sweet-feed" which is a molasses-soaked grain. Sweet feed is a little like ice cream or chocolate for horses. Diamond, the white horse, will eat the alfalfa until she sees me removing the top from the sweet-feed container, then she will simply stand there looking at me, as if I was teasing with the alfalfa! She will reluctantly return to the alfalfa when she finishes the sweet feed.

Ritzi the Morgan has a similar routine but is a more enthusiastic eater, so he doesn't stop tucking into the alfalfa until the actual second that the sweet-feed container arrives, then he does a quick-shift over to the new stuff without taking a breath.

Chick ignores the sweet feed! She will even keep eating the alfalfa while the goats steal her sweet-feed! She shows no interest at all. Very strange to me! It's a bit like an 8-year-old saying "No chocolate cereal for me, give me more dry toast!"

I have to say that Chick is very elegant. She needs a good home, has been ridden and needs some love and training. By the way, Ritzi needs a home too in the near future. He came to us looking terrible but is very healthy now. He is a Morgan.

Well, after the feeding routine, it's time for work.

Postscript: All these beauties did get new homes.

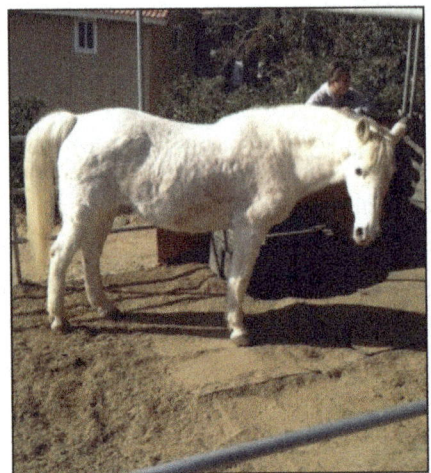

Diamond

Ritzi

Chick

2 Beautiful Horses

In 2014 we took in 2 beautiful white horses at the same time from different places. Desi was an Andalusian and Cruze was the other. They seemed to like each other!

Chapter 23

HAY IS DANGEROUS

Whenever I say "Hay!" I have an irresistible urge to sing "Hey, hey we're the Monkees"! If you are over a certain age the song will now be going around in your head for the rest of the day; my apologies for that. Those under a certain age probably think this is some sort of zoological reference from an animal rescue guy who has "lost it".

Well, back to my headline. Hay is dangerous!

As you know by now, at Modjeska Ranch Rescue, we usually have a number of horses, some goats and some pigs and part of my morning routine is to feed them, top up their water, clean up all the dog poop and generally help out while Teresa feeds dogs and cats, medicates such things as diabetic dogs, rheumatic dogs, dogs with "Cushings", cats with UTIs (urinary tract infections) and animals with other illnesses or just old dogs and cats with aches and pains.

The other day I went into the hay shed to gather hay to feed the horses and goats. There was no loose hay, so I had to cut a new bale. For those of you unfamiliar with this (as was I until 20 years ago), hay bales are held together with 3 strands of twine, pulled so tight that you must dig for it. Well, it was early, so I grabbed a sharp knife and started to saw away at the first strand of twine. I didn't seem to be making the usual progress...it shouldn't take long! Suddenly I saw blood pouring down my finger! As I said, it was very early. I had the knife the wrong way round with my finger pressing down on the sharp blade! No wonder it wasn't cutting the twine, it was cutting my finger! I made some appropriate exclamation of surprise and pain to which I am sure the horses said, "Where is my food" and "Don't give me the bit with the blood on". The cut took a while to heal. I will try to wake up before doing this in the future.

Hay has other dangerous properties. It may seem surprising, but it is quite possible to get splinters from grabbing a flake of hay. This is why you see sensible people, not me I might add, wear gloves to handle it. I tend to grab a flake in each hand and then curse when a tiny sliver works its way under my skin or even worse under my fingernail. As with most splinters the removal process can be more painful than their entry and sometimes takes days.

Another dangerous property of hay is its weight. When you see a cowboy sling a bale of hay up on a truck, it is the result of strength and technique. Most hay bales around here weigh 100 lbs although some are 120 lbs. I defy you to just lift it without severe physical risk. If the hay delivery guy cannot get the hay where you want it, the safest way to move it is on a "dolly" or cut into smaller bales. I have lifted/dragged/manhandled full bales on occasion through sheer frustration or impatience and I do not recommend it for those who are not on an Olympic training regime or who value their back.

Hay is also dangerous to one's bank account. The severe drought in many parts of the US together with the conversion of hay fields to corn for ethanol (thankfully abating), has seen the price of hay spike over the last few years. We used to pay $12 a bale. At the time of writing, it is around $25 a bale (and at the time of editing it is $34 a bale) If you are feeding 5 or 6 horses every day, that makes a big difference to the budget. You can get hay cheaper if you drive a way to get it, have a truck on which to load it and will buy 40 or 50 bales at once. We do not have a truck and do not have a place to store 40 or 50 bales of hay safely.

Hay can also cause arguments. OK let's be PC and call them honest disagreements. If you ask 5 different horse people how much you should feed a particular horse and what type of hay, you will get 7 different answers (like asking a question of 7 lawyers). Alfalfa, Orchard, Bermuda, three-way, pellets, sweet-feed, vitamin supplements etc etc. Feed twice a day, three times a day, one type or a mixture....it befuddles my mind. Fortunately, I do not make those decisions; Teresa makes them after consultation with our many knowledgeable horse community friends. I just do as I am told which is much easier.

Hay can also be dangerous if it is stored wet. A stack of hay bales that is wet can generate heat and spontaneously combust. Apparently, this can happen if the moisture content is more than about 20%. This is not a big issue around here of course, but it is certainly a reason not to allow hay to get wet when it does rain.

So horse life can be complicated and dangerous. We have survived at the Rescue so far with only one serious injury. One of our few volunteers moved a very heavy rubber mat into the corral to a place where it got wet but was mostly hidden by shavings and hay. Teresa walked into the corral and tripped on the wet mat and broke her ankle very badly, a double vertical fracture. She was on a scooter and in a boot for some time but fortunately made a full recovery. Full story in another chapter.

I hope these warnings will help YOU stay safe around dangerous hay!!

Labradors

A labyrinth of lovely Labradors. These Labs all came into Modjeska Ranch Rescue in a period of two weeks. Barbie and Old Yeller came in separately and Chewbacca and Lacey came in together. They are all "mature" but not old and just follow us around as a foursome all wanting to be petted all the time. Petting just one for more than 5 seconds is impossible as the others pile in.

It is strange but now and again we seem to take in a lot of one breed. One year we took a lot of huskies, another year St Bernards, and always Great Danes. I don't have an explanation for this.

Chapter 24

RAINDROPS KEEP FALLING ON MY ROOF AND BLACK BEAUTY GOES TO THE BIG KENNEL IN THE SKY

I know we need rain. That H2O stuff seems essential to life, or at least that's what the scientists tell us when they analyze far off planets and asteroids. BTW wouldn't asteroids be a better word for Hemorrhoids? Sorry for the random non-PC thought!

One thing we usually rely on is to have some kind of shelter over our essential belongings and ideally ourselves, unless of course we are British, in which case standing in the rain is a perfectly normal daily occurrence, as you wait for the bus that is half an hour late which then drives straight past you at the bus-stop because it is full of people who have been standing in the rain at an earlier stop. There is a certain smell to being in a crowd of very wet people on a bus. Memories of my youth! Now living in Orange County for 35 years, I admit to never having been on a bus in that time.

At Modjeska Ranch Rescue, we have a garage with a flat roof. Well, in theory it is not flat. It is sloped very slightly to allow the wonders of gravity to remove rainfall effortlessly from the roof and onto the driveway. For those of you who have enjoyed a "flat" roof, that last sentence will have raised a chuckle of mirth and perhaps stirred up a few painful memories.

The "flat" roof on top of our garage has been patched with all sorts of miracle products, painted with "guaranteed" easy to apply coatings, re-covered three times with traditional roofing material and, pause for mirth again, covered with blue and green tarpaulins on many occasions which must be tied down as our heavy rains are often accompanied by very high winds.

Of course, being Southern California, there is never a car in this garage with the flat roof. It is full of dog and cat crates, supplies, food, tools, blankets, towels, comforters and dog and cat beds. By the way, when I wrote this, I drove a black car which had to stay out in the sun so the special expensive, guaranteed, clearcoat paint protector totally peeled off and it looked ghastly! What a waste of money.

Back to the roof! The flat roof extends not only over the garage but also over my office in the house, and the bar area in the family room. As I said I have had the roof fixed a couple of times but last winter it leaked again, into the garage, into the office, and into the bar! In addition to rain and sun, this flat roof must stand up to the pounding given to it by a lot of dogs. There is a door to the flat area/patio over the garage directly from our bedroom, and the dogs have access to this area at night and often at other times, as you will remember that the dogs live in the house at Modjeska Ranch, not in cages and crates! At night-time the dog's easiest access for their necessary functions is the flat garage roof. (OK I already know you think we are crazy to which I plead no contest)

This year I determined to fix the roof, and "fix it good". This year we would NOT have leaks! They drive me crazy.

It had been a warm summer and in mid-September I started to strip the roof, check the wood for soundness, and replace any wood that needed it. I took plenty of advice on how to do this right. This is an area about 23 feet wide by 30 feet long! I discovered a number of things during this process (you may want to take notes for future reference)

- 8 foot by 4 foot, ¾ inch plywood sheathing is very heavy!
- It is unwieldy and difficult to manhandle alone!
- It can shove painful splinters up behind your fingernails (note to self, wear gloves!)
- The old wood you are removing has nails in it and it is inadvisable to stand on them as they go through your shoes and into your foot.
- If you work on the roof without a shirt and bend over a lot, that lower waistline at the bottom of your back can get very sunburnt and it is painful!

I spent a few days making good progress, sometimes with help from my son-in-law. A few days ago, I had reached the point where I had replaced a large area of rotten wood, sealed lots of gaps with "trowel patch" and stripped waterproof covering from other areas ready to re-cover the roof completely with black paper and roofing material and sealant.

The times I can spend on the roof are dictated by the needs of my clients in my Real Estate business. I had been very busy which is a good thing!). The weather has been good, so no panics there.

Until Wednesday October 9th!

I saw the forecast for a few light sprinkles of rain, but thought it was not a problem. Well, "the heavens opened". Lashing rain! Both Teresa and

I were working. We returned home to find the garage, the bar area and the office very wet!! Supplies in the garage were also wet but fortunately some of it was covered by tarps, so it could have been worse.

Our initial reaction was frustration expressed loudly with the use of very bad language. Does that paint the right picture? While I am working on the garage into which water has leaked, the garage lights also decide not to work, so we were thrashing around in the semi-dark with flashlights trying to save what we could of the supplies in the garage. We had to throw away a lot of dog food. It was not a happy sight, and we were not having a happy family conversation!

Anyway, the weather had improved, and I hoped to get the roof finished before the next downpour.

On top of this, we had had a sad morning. Black Beauty was an old black racing Greyhound rescue. She had lived at the Rescue for probably 5 years. She was very old, with an almost completely grey face. She kept herself to herself and loved to sleep on the bed, sometimes even trying to get between us. When we were not looking and not in bed Black Beauty would get on our bed and paw away at the comforter to get underneath and lie directly on all the pillows which drives me crazy as I hate anything like that around my face. It doesn't bother Teresa at all.

Well, on Wednesday morning, we woke up and Black Beauty was lying at the foot of the bed on my feet. There were 3 other dogs on the bed at the time, a French Bulldog, a Great Dane and a Standard Poodle. We rolled out of bed, but Black Beauty did not move. It took us a couple of minutes to realize that she was dead as she was capable of lying in that position all day if we allowed it. She was very old, and died very peacefully, so we should not really be sad, but it was a little strange without that crotchety old girl slinking around the place. RIP Black Beauty.

Postscript: The garage continued to leak a little after my efforts. The answer of course was to get a professional roofer to fix it properly, but we simply could not afford that, as I had quotes of $10,000-$15,000 and we just didn't have it. Also, the railings around that upstairs patio were old, rotted wood with 8 inch gaps, which were not only not up to current safety codes but also coming to pieces. We had metal X-Pens attached to the pillars to keep the dogs safe. It did not look attractive at all. Again, replacing the railings was beyond our financial means.

The huge "Header" wood beam which is over the double garage door started to sag. It is about 12 inches deep, 6 inches wide and 23 feet long, just a huge piece of wood. The leaks had led to it starting to collapse. Something had to be done. A good friend in the canyon who owns a framing business arranged to replace the header for us which was great as he paid for it and made sure it was done properly. The structure was now safe. However, in order to get it in, the stucco had to be removed from around the door. It was now safe, but ugly. I got quotes to replace the stucco and again they were crazy, one quote was $6,000 for about 80 square feet of stucco.

Five years later, with support from a generous donor who paid for about half of the project, we had a professional roofer fix the garage roof/patio, a metalworking company install new railings and a contractor friend found someone to replace the stucco. Finally, we have a patio/garage roof, really nice new railings and new stucco and a new garage door. We are delighted and grateful for all the help given to us to get this done.

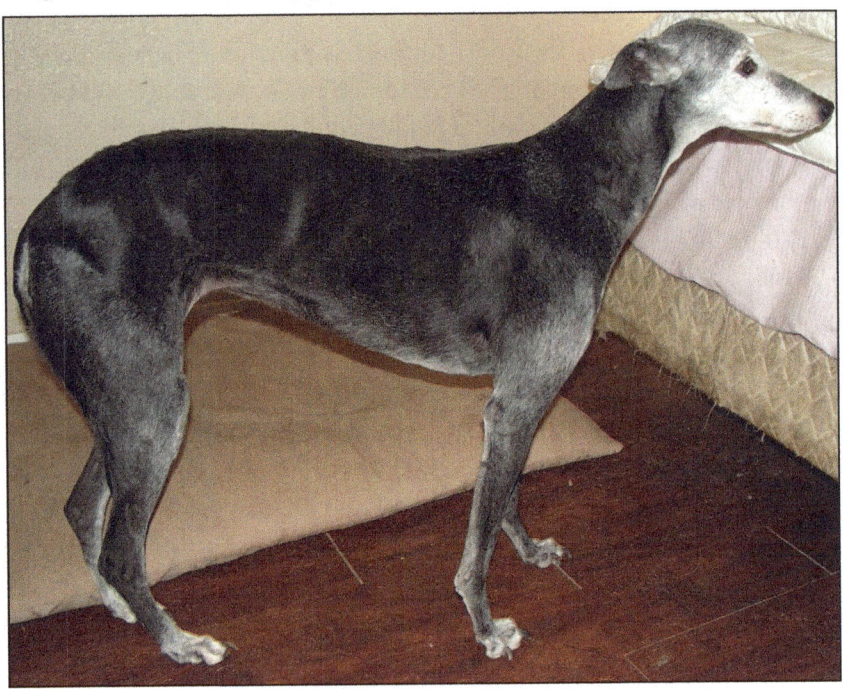

Black Beauty

A Modjeska Kitchen Scene

Waiting for breakfast. "Hey feed us now, you can blow leaves later". Bella, whose story you can read elsewhere in the book, is in the background sharing the couch with Rambo. Rocky the Collie is at the front. Rocky's fur was so thick you could brush him for hours and end up with piles of fur. He would groom himself too and have strands of fur caught in his teeth. We told him to floss but he didn't obey.

Chapter 25

I JUST SPENT HALF AN HOUR ON THE FLOOR WITH TERESA

When I was much younger, half an hour on the floor with the woman I love was something I had to plan and scheme to achieve; especially before I had my own place! Well, hey, I was young once, despite the belief of my children that I was born at the age of 35 and am more interested in football than romance.

Anyway, I digress.

One of the realities of life in a Rescue where over half of the animals we care for are old, is that they have "issues". Not people-type issues about who should empty the dishwasher, or who doesn't know how to load it properly; I still haven't managed to get a dog to load its bowl into the dishwasher at all, or even make an attempt! I do know a Vet who had trained her dog to open the fridge door and bring her a beer!

Anyway, we had a dog with some ailments that required a certain amount of solitude and peace and I challenge you to find that in a house with 25 dogs. This dog did not want to eat or drink much and was in a large dog enclosure with lots of blankets and towels for comfort. We knew she needed to eat and drink but was not inclined to do so. A look from her hooded eyes while she sat on the donated blankets almost said "REEAALLY!!!!.........And you want me to eat!! OK, humans, imagine you have the flu, and a hangover...and someone says you need to eat......what do you tell them!!??"

Of course, she doesn't have the flu and a hangover but I think that's the drift of the "look".

So, Teresa and I are on the floor with the dog, trying to tempt her to eat food which, of course, has medication hidden in it. I can almost hear the dog laughing "You expect me to fall for that old one!"

There are pills in the food, squirty liquids in a syringe to squirt into her mouth, and all the while we are stroking her and murmuring completely crazy reassurances into the dog's ear.

A sick dog, lying on nice comfy blankets, tends not to get up so often to do what dogs do...so the blankets need changing often...lovely smelly job.

I spent how many years at college to pick up yucky blankets and try to get them outside with minimum damage to my clothing and surroundings? Ha...life is a strange journey!

Since she is not going out much, we washed her down with warm damp towels, so she felt clean and cared for. I wish someone would do that for me!

The other dogs of course want to get in on the act. This one is getting so much attention, it's not fair, and is getting smelly wet food when they only get dry food. So, while scrabbling about on the floor we also must run interference on those dogs who have managed to evade whatever general protection barriers we have erected. There are never enough.

An exciting romantic night at Modjeska Rescue on the floor with my wife is not all it seems. Those of you with a few animals may be able to relate.

We could always retire to our romantic bedroom where at least 5 dogs will expect to be on the bed with us and they will expect to receive any hugs and kisses that are on offer! Those longing eyes gazing over the pillow tend to be exclusively canine!

Pixie and Mooshoo, 2 French citizens living in California

Modjeska Ranch Rescue has great couches!

My name is Stevie and I am the most interesting cat in the world!

Chapter 26

TERESA BREAKS HER ANKLE AND I FALL OVER A DOG

It has been an eventful time at Modjeska Ranch Rescue. A few weeks ago, I stood in the kitchen leaning against the island sipping a glass of wine while talking to Teresa who had just got home from work and also needed wine.

Unbeknownst to me, Rocky the large black Collie had settled down centimeters behind my feet.

I am very expressive when I talk, using my hands and movement to emphasize whatever my latest jewels of insight may be. As I attempted to take a small step backwards, the path of my foot was impeded by a very solid Collie, which caused me to fall backwards, my head just missing our other bar-height kitchen island, but my left hand was put out to break my fall, or as it turned out, to almost break my hand as I plummeted to the hard tile floor on my back. My tailbone and my hand took the brunt of the fall, and I lay there for a couple of minutes moaning while Teresa tried to get me up. I did not want to move as I felt like I had been run over by a truck. I hasten to add that my fall was not a result of the aforementioned wine!

My tailbone was bruised and painful for a week, but my hand still hurt some weeks later although fortunately was not broken. Enough to say that during the incident, Rocky did not move an inch! I could not lift anything heavy with that hand for a long time. I was scheduled to play golf with my Son-in-law. Missing golf is a major tragedy as I get to play rarely, and very badly.

As if this was not enough drama, about 2 weeks later we had another accident. Jesse is our farrier, and a neighbor, who tends to the feet of our horses. I was away from the house at work and knew that Jesse was at our house with a couple of people helping him. I arrived home from work and was confused. Jesse's truck was in the driveway, there were a couple of guys hanging around that I didn't recognize, and I could see Teresa inside on the couch. Normally if anyone arrives or is working with the animals, she would be out with them "supervising".

It turned out that these guys had just carried Teresa inside. They had all been in the corral and Teresa slipped on a heavy thick rubber mat that was wet. Her ankle was badly swollen. We left it overnight but then went for X-Rays and found that she had 2 vertical fractures of the ankle. This was very painful. The Doctor put a splint on it and made an appointment with the orthopedic specialist. Teresa had to have a cast from toe to knee and wait 3 weeks until they knew whether it needed surgery.

This presented several challenges:

Teresa could not move around well, she still wanted to go to work, she still wanted to feed the animals, it was her right foot so she couldn't drive, and she is a horrible passenger, showering and dressing was very difficult, so we bought her a waterproof boot for showering which was still a challenge, the dogs all wanted to climb on the couch with her and she was in pain.

Teresa is a very self-contained person. She doesn't need anyone to help her in everyday life, she just gets it done. However, a broken ankle proved to be a significant barrier to some activities. For the first few days Teresa hobbled about on crutches, but even she would admit to not being a great athlete on crutches, and she struggled to get around. One day at work she toppled over into an island display of potty pads at the pet supply store! I wish I had video of that!

So, time for the "Scooter". We bought a kneel-on scooter, which proved to be a very useful machine! Teresa "scooted" around like a race driver and was able to do 80% of what she normally does. So, there are still lots of chores to be done, animals to feed, poop to be scooped, medications to be given, floors to be cleaned, washing to be done, blanket/sheet/towel/food donations to be sorted. Oh, and of course, we both have to go to work for a living as well.........

Feeding the cats, horses and goats is my usual routine, so no problem. Feeding the dogs is an exercise in military discipline and coordination. During Teresa's time in the foot-cast, I would bring in the dry food from our storage area (often erroneously called a garage but this is California), and the wet food from a cabinet. Teresa balanced herself on the "scooter" between the stove and the island and arranged the bowls of various sizes into which she poured dry dog food, and usually mixed in some wet food, and/or some grated cheese. She mixes it all and then there are various piles of bowls. I take 5 dogs to one area and close a baby-gate; 3 out in the front and close the door, and then about 12 more in and around the kitchen/family room, then a couple upstairs. Some of the bowls have medication so it is important to observe who is eating what. Often the medication is fed by hand with either "Philly" or peanut butter. The Bulldogs must go outside with one of the Danes, as the Bulldogs will want all the food. They are not aggressive with the other dogs, they just sort of nuzzle in underneath them and nudge them out of the way. Scooby is the biggest/tallest Dane, but he is a softie, and while the other dogs dive in, Scooby will circle the food looking up at me for approval "Woo...is that REALLY for me ??"

We move the dogs around sometimes depending on the "mix" at the time. For a few days, one of the older Danes was fed in our bedroom with a couple of the other dogs. One day, I had not changed out of my business clothes yet, so before feeding I went to the bedroom to change. Unfortunately, one of the very old Danes had climbed on the bed and peed so I saw that and pulled off the comforter, then slipped on the poop I had not seen which she had also left on the floor! I got a little frustrated and tried to take off my pooped shoes and managed to get my shoelaces in a knot so I could not take them off! I was hopping around the bedroom with poop on my shoe and knotted laces. Such is the excitement of animal rescue! The good news is that Teresa's 3-week check-up resulted in the cast coming off and the Doctor remarking on how well she had healed. Then she had a "boot" on which she could walk, and drive! That was a blessing to all concerned.

Fortunately, some years later Teresa's foot seems to be fine, and so are my tailbone and wrist.

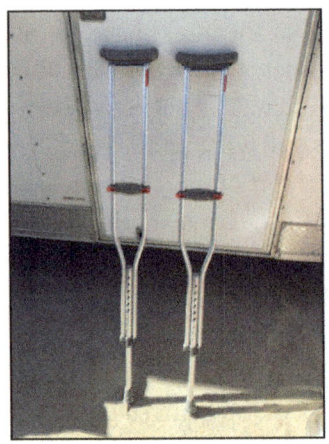

Teresa's walking aids

Hanging out in the kitchen, maybe there is food

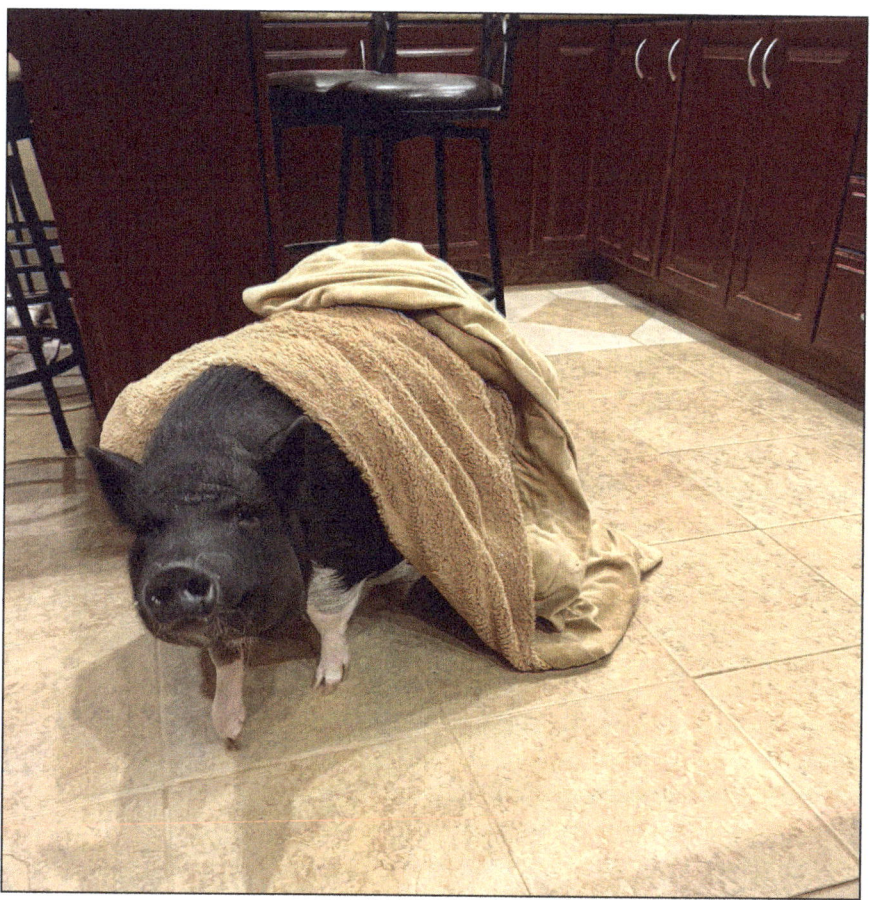

Polly the pig is fun to have around

Chapter 27

MOVING THE PIG

We did not plan to have pigs.

In fact, the "ambulatory bacon" history started on Nikki's 8th birthday in 2001. We also had a 12-year-old foster daughter at the time (we had fostered many children over the years but that's a different book). Anyway, Nikki told Teresa that she wanted a pet pig for her birthday. I have no idea where the idea came from, but Teresa decided that if Nikki was getting a pig then our foster daughter could have one too.

At this point, I had not been consulted on the issue. I can hear husbands across the world nodding in understanding and women saying, "Why would she ask you anyway?"

Teresa did eventually ask me in her wonderful "fait accompli" way. She called me at work and explained how the girls wanted a pig each and how did I feel about that, as if it mattered. I reluctantly agreed and made one stipulation. "Not in the house!". "OK" said Teresa.

I arrived home to find the 2 one-foot-long piglets in my office at the house.

"Well, it's cold outside," said Teresa.

"They are pigs" I said.

"Well, they can go outside when it's warmer and they've grown a bit. They're only babies"

That of course meant they were "inside" pigs.

Well, here's an education for you. In the absence of something else handy, pigs will eat anything, including drywall. Small pigs will go under desks and chairs, and behind cabinets and bookshelves....and eat drywall. They will literally eat holes in the wall.

Teresa thought this was amusing. I did not share her mirth.

A little later, after some persuasion on my part, the pigs went out to their own large, fenced area in which we built little houses for them in case in rained.

The pigs grew. Whilst the generally held perception of pot belly pigs is that they are small, there is a little-known phenomenon. If you feed them, they grow. A fully grown pot belly, while not rivaling a 600 lb Gloucester

Spot, can easily tip the scales at 100-150lbs. We also put a kid's plastic bathing pool in the pig area as they love to roll around in the water which is instantly black.

They also like to fornicate. Pigs have interesting habits; the male pig's member is long and curly. They can orgasm for 30 minutes! Now who wants to be a pig?

For a while we stationed a small fence enclosure in the driveway. It was there because a couple of police officers we know would call us after night shift and drop off stray animals they had found.

One day Teresa and I had been somewhere, and we got back to find a very large pig in the enclosure. After investigation we still have no idea where it came from.

We couldn't leave it in the driveway so decided it had to go up the hill into the big field, about 75 yards. We had something to eat in the kitchen while we debated a pig-move strategy. In the meantime, the pig got out of the enclosure in the driveway and proceeded to run around the yard while we ran after, and in front of, him trying to make sure he didn't run into the street and cause an accident. Eventually we coaxed him back into the enclosure which was still 75 yards from where we wanted him.

The only problem was that neither of us had a clue how to move a pig. Being dog people, we eventually got a leash around its neck and another around its middle which was large as the pig must have weighed 150-200 lbs.

We encouraged the pig to move in the indicated direction with gentle tugs on the leash. Nothing. We pulled harder. Nothing. Finally, with both of us pulling, the pig moved...about a foot. The task was not made easier by the fact that I was not wearing sensible shoes but was wearing thongs, the type you wear on the beach, no, not a stripper thong but the kind you put on your feet, and I used to call flip-flops.

We progressed therefore a foot at a time halfway to the destination. We were exhausted and the pig was squealing like, well, a stuck pig. The neighbors must have thought we were killing this pig. The leash around its neck had slid up around its ears and this was not good, but we couldn't go back.

The whole process took an hour of pushing, pulling and squealing.

We eventually had 7 pigs.

Would you like a pig?

Chapter 28

POM IN BATHROOM AND TARANTULAS

Living in an animal rescue daily, as a married couple, with one's own offspring, may evoke visions of smiling faces and jolly animals having fun, but it is occasionally more akin to a madhouse. It can also strain the "understanding" between family members!

Of course, family comes first, although Teresa has elicited looks of horror from some animal community friends when she says this as there are plenty of people with strange views in all walks of life. Despite this, the needs of the humans in our house are often relegated to the bottom of the list, and even forgotten completely, as the needs of the animals seem to take up all the time and energy available in any one day.

On arriving home after a hard day at work, many normal families start to prepare dinner, maybe sit down for half an hour, maybe pour a glass of wine or open a beer or have a cup of tea. In our house there are animal chores to be done before we can relax, because it is impossible for us to relax unless the animals are relaxed. That usually means they must be fed, and the blankets, beds and floors must be checked for pee, poop, throw-up etc. and all of them checked to make sure they do not seem to be ailing with anything.

One of the things that can send Teresa into a tailspin is Tarantulas in the house! Once there were two of them in the hallway by the front door. Teresa is terrified of Tarantulas. I admit they look scary, but they are not dangerous, so I put something like a plastic food container over them, slide a piece of card underneath and take them outside and over the road to the hillside. I think Teresa would rather take more drastic action.

Another thing I thought might be contentious and a subject for "lively debate" was that I was supposed to be paying especially close attention to an old Pomeranian which was in our bedroom for some reason. Well, somehow, he managed to go into our master bathroom and close the door, and then the door handle chose that moment to become inoperative. I turned it, shook it, banged the door, but nothing would budge the door from its closed condition!

I considered various ways that Teresa would kill me for stranding this dog in the bathroom. Fortunately, she was not home. I was in the fast science stream in school and passed "A" level (advanced level for you non-Brits) Mathematics, Physics and Chemistry exams at the age of 17. So I put all that scientific knowledge into effect and kicked the door down with my foot, breaking it off its hinges. The dog was fine.

Kong the Pom that I locked in the bathroom

What time does Santa get here

Chapter 29

LLAMALAND

When the fires raged in Modjeska Canyon in 2007, Jim and Diane's house across the street tragically burned down, trapped between 2 advancing pincers of the fire. Their great geodesic dome house, a local landmark, didn't have a chance and all that was left was an ash-strewn concrete slab.

During TV coverage of the fire, which almost reached a paparazzi-frenzy, many of the TV stations opened their coverage with a shot of Llamas bouncing around the burned hillsides. These Llamas belonged to Jim and Diane.

Jim and Diane had acquired the Llamas for that age-old reason, it seemed like a good idea at the time, they liked Llamas, and they keep down the brush on the steep hillside behind the house. Having land, for those who lust after some and don't have any, is WORK! Llamas keeping down the brush sounds good to me, and they cope well with the steep terrain.

Well, eventually animal control managed to get hold of the llamas and took them to the County Fairground. Llamas don't travel well and don't like confinement or new places. They stress easily. They are pretty but not bright. One of the Llamas died in the process, not from abuse but just probably stress.

Teresa knew the people at the Fairground very well and had said we would help wherever we could. Jim and Diane asked if we would take the 3 remaining llamas to Modjeska Ranch until they could rebuild their house. Well, those of you who have tried to build a house in Orange County will know that the regulations are tight. It took a long time to get planning permission and build their new house, which is very beautiful. The llamas lived at Modjeska Ranch for over two years. They are beautiful beasts, but they can spit what seems like ten egg yolks a long way! They did get on well with all our other outside animals and were a fun addition to the family for a while.

Chapter 30

HURRICANE KATRINA

Hurricane Katrina was a Category 5 tropical cyclone in August 2005, which caused $125 billion in damage, particularly in the city of New Orleans and the surrounding areas, and an estimated 1833 deaths. It was the costliest tropical cyclone on record, tying now with Hurricane Harvey in 2017. (Wikipedia)

The Federal Government and FEMA (the Federal Emergency Management Authority) have plans for dealing with emergencies like hurricanes, but in the instance of Katrina, it seemed that the response was hampered by its unexpected size, collapse of some of the levies, and turf-wars between Federal, State and City government. There was a lot of chaos. Large areas of the city were flooded, people and animals were on roofs, in boats etc. Lots of people were trying to help I am sure but there was a lot of confusion.

One of the problems that only really became publicly apparent later was that the rule apparently for the official rescuers in boats was "People, not animals". Rescue boats would take people but not animals, a guideline since changed I believe.

During Katrina some people would not get into rescue boats and abandon their animals even though they were waist deep in water or on the roof of a house. Others were forced to be "rescued" and leave behind their pets, causing anguish on top of grief. I am sure lots of people were doing their best to help but it was total chaos for some time.

Many of the rescued people were taken to the Superdome. For those of you unfamiliar with New Orleans, a wonderful place by the way, the Superdome is a huge indoor football and exhibition hall/stadium which had cots lined up for homeless people. However, the facilities were said to be simply unable to cope with the numbers. People from all over the country went down to Louisiana to help.

Animal organizations around the country started to get involved because there was no clear plan to deal with the thousands of animals left alone and stranded, either wading in the streets or sitting on roofs isolated by flooding.

An enterprising group of people arranged to airlift some of the animals to other parts of the country as the New Orleans animal facilities were overwhelmed. One of those airlifts brought cats and dogs to Los Angeles where many rescues organizations had volunteered to help, all organized by a lady whose name is on the tip of my tongue.

Modjeska Ranch Rescue took several vans and volunteers up to a warehouse near Los Angeles airport on the designated day of arrival. The warehouse was huge and filled with dogs and cats in travel crates. We got there very early and registered to take about 6 dogs I seem to remember. It was a very long day, and we were about the last organization to leave, having been begged to take some of the ones that no one else wanted to take, so we ended up with 10 dogs and 4 cats, driving away in the dark after about 10 hours of warehouse time.

One of the challenges posed by this new intake was that heartworm is very common in the South where it is humid, but not very common at all in California where it is dry. We found that several the dogs had heartworm, which can shorten a dog's life and damage organs. Treating heartworm takes time and is expensive. We had to keep the dogs in special kennels we built in the garage and take them out often on a leach so we could make sure they didn't get bitten by a mosquito and spread the disease. Because of this it took some time to treat the infected dogs before we could find them a new home.

One of the controversial issues at the time was that, by removing the animals from their local area, it made reuniting them with their original owners almost impossible. We were asked to keep the dogs a period of time in case owners came forward. How people would get in touch in such a chaotic situation was a big question. Remember, amazing as it may seem, this was 2 years before the first IPhone came out.

The internet as it was then did find 2 cat owners and 1 dog owner who thought we may have their animals. After some back and forth, we determined that the dog owner was looking for a different dog, but the cat owners were right!

We shipped the cats back to New Orleans. One of them arrived on Christmas Day and was met at the airport by the owner who called us in floods of tears as she was so happy. That was a small silver lining to a terrible tragedy. All the other animals eventually found new homes in nice DRY California

Some of the 2005 Katrina rescues including a Mom with pups born at Modjeska, the brown one lying down in my office. One of the pups was adopted by a friend so we saw him grow up.

By Russell Taylor

The Living Room at Modjeska Ranch Rescue

Not much room for humans and yes that's Polly the pig

Chapter 31
SAYING NO AND INTAKE REASONS

The hardest thing in the 20 years of building and running a Rescue is saying "No we can't take another one at this time".

We get requests every day to take in animals of various types and ages in a range of conditions, from very good to really bad shape. The stories attached to the animal are often heart-breaking and can take half an hour on the phone to hear. The stories attached to the human giving up the animal can also be tough to hear, but then again some of them are laughably unbelievable or really annoying.

When we started, most of our dogs and cats were adoptable, so when they got adopted, a space opened up for another rescue intake.

In later years of the Rescue, we have gradually become three-quarters full with long-term rescues, becoming a hospice or sanctuary for animals with nowhere else to go. This means that it becomes harder for us to take in new rescues because spaces open up more rarely. If they are old and do not get adopted, that space doesn't open up until they pass away. We have dogs who have been here over ten years.

Whereas in our early days we may have taken in new animals every week, the hospice-model rescue in later years might take in one or two a month, sometimes three or four. This is often not understood by the desperate people who call us every day, who have often already been turned down by multiple other rescues. Sometimes we can help by networking with other rescues who may have space and often just giving the time to talk and discuss their situation can help, although I assure you that sometimes, after a day's work, our reservoir of nervous energy and physical stamina needed for these conversations is running at a low ebb.

A question we are often asked relates to what is our capacity, for how many dogs, cats etc do we have room? I'm sure to many that seems like a simple question, and in some rescues or shelters maybe it is. If you keep the dogs and cats in kennels and runs, then your capacity may be however many runs/kennels you have, although it also may not.

Our capacity is not a number. We do have a legal limit set by our county license, but the more relevant information is the age, health, size and temperament of the dogs we have. 35 dogs with no medical issues who are low energy and like to lay on the couch all day is one scenario. 35 dogs who are blind, diabetic, have cancer, are 6 months old and hyperactive or anti-social, or have trouble controlling their bowels is a completely different scenario.

Add to that whether we ourselves are feeling great or feeling overwhelmed or sick. Our capacity is fluid and we do not appreciate "helpful" advice on what we should or should not do or take in. Occasionally we are tempted to suggest that if it's so easy, why don't YOU do it, but that wouldn't achieve anything or help the animal...although it might feel good!

We can't save them all. As said earlier when we cannot take an animal, we often try hard to share needs to other rescues and animal lovers. There are many emails, Facebook posts, Instagram posts and FB messages every day circulating between different organizations, but we all face the same problems of capacity, finance and exhaustion.

The most frustrating conversations are those where someone is giving up an animal for reasons that leave us annoyed. There are times when we can understand and sympathize with the distressed owner, but the following are just some of the reasons given to us which is why Teresa says she doesn't like people very much:

- "We are moving to a new house, and we don't want this Labrador on the new carpet!". Yes, we were told this.
- "We got the dog while the kids were young, but now they have gone to college and we want to travel, the dog has got to go"
- "We didn't realize German Shepherds/Great Danes/any other dog breed got so big."
- "We got the dog a couple of years ago but now we want to start a family and don't want a dog around the baby."
- The dogs are getting old, and the kids want a puppy. We were told in this way, a couple pulled into our driveway in their Lexus SUV, got out with their 2 children maybe 6 or 7 years old and their 2 older terriers which they had owned since puppies. Having given us the dogs with some sad story and everyone being in tears, the younger child turned to his mom and said "Can we go and get the puppy now?"
- We took in a 4-month-old Dalmatian many years ago, at the request of neighbors and Police. It had a broken leg. The owner had become annoyed when the puppy peed on the white bedroom carpet and had thrown it out of a second story window! (Note: if you don't want

puppy pee in your bedroom, don't have the puppy unsupervised in your bedroom)

- We took in a hound mix that had been tied to a fence by the exit ramp of the 5 Freeway. The dog's front leg was tied up, so it was above his heart. We don't know how long he had been there, but it was long enough for the leg to be severely starved of blood. Despite Vet efforts, the leg had to be amputated. It may surprise you that three days later he was running around the yard on 3 legs as if there was nothing wrong.

- When we get calls/emails/texts from people wanting us to take an animal and we cannot take them, most people are understanding and thankful for our advice as to what to do next. However, some are indignant, "You are a rescue, you HAVE to take him, we are leaving tomorrow, and he has to be gone. I'll report you!" I am not sure who they think they will report us to, but some people have the impression that we are somehow taxpayer supported, which of course we are not, we survive from donations and our own pocket.

- Other people call us wanting to adopt, which is a nicer call to get but I would say the ratio is 20:1 in the other direction. Most of these people are very courteous and sometimes we have something that will interest them. Occasionally however we feel looked upon as the Nordstrom/Harrods/Bloomingdales pet department and we are spoken down to by people who want to give us a breed, shape, size, color, temperament order as if we have a rack of dogs with size and price labels on them. The primary motivation seems to be to get a $2000 dog cheap, as opposed to rescuing a new furry friend. By the way we do get a lot of pure breed dogs despite many thinking we just have "mixes". I would say 75% of the dogs we have had are pure bred.

Don't get the wrong idea. There are lots of supporters and genuine people in need of our help who totally understand what we do and how hard it is, and many have become friends and cheerleaders, but I wanted to give you a flavor of the other side of the coin. On a day which has been full of the difficult disheartening people, one is sometimes tempted to just say "******* it, I've had enough, it's time to retire".

If I shuffle about enough I can get all of me on here!

Chapter 32

COUCH TIME -AS A DOG IN 2016!!!!!!

In a dog Voice for an email which we sent out:

It was cold and windy over in Modjeska Canyon at Christmas in 2016 and we just fought over space on one of the couches. Those silly humans kept cleaning up outside and inside which is totally pointless in the wind which blew all the plants over, ripped up the artificial grass, and broke branches off the trees. The wind in Modjeska gathers speed over the hill and was 100 mph plus. The couch is the place to be... but since we are all on them those humans will have to sit on the floor! Anyway, they need to exercise after all that eating they did!!

Hannah showing her yoga moves on the couch

Cody, Shamu, Dotch and Pixie. Dotch came to us from a hoarder and had only one tooth but he is very happy and eats everything in sight.

By Russell Taylor

Bella, Scooby and Rambo looking guilty

Chapter 33

BILLY GOT OUT!

Billy got out! This morning, we were in the kitchen and Teresa was fixing the morning dog food bowls. Suddenly she looked out of the window and shouted, "Billy is out!". We have 3 goats in the corral and field. Billy is the smallest and quite a fun guy, but he does have horns, so care is needed. Anyway, he was very cooperative and, as you can see below, followed Teresa back into the corral quite easily, giving a quick glance to the camera for his hall of fame picture. The next job was to find HOW he got out. As you may know I like to eat dry cereal for breakfast, but this morning Teresa scattered my dry cereal all over the corral to keep the goats occupied while we found the unauthorized exit. I will have to eat later.

We found a hole low down in the fence and managed to fix it with a mixture of wire and tie-wraps.

Fixing this fence follows the previous day when I had to fix the fence between the dogs and the pigs which had been undermined by a digging dog whose identity remains in doubt.

Billy

Chapter 34

THE COLD EQUATION AND LIFE

(written before my Mom passed away and before we installed huge dog doors in 2019 allowing us to keep doors closed when it is cold)

It's been cold the last few days! That presents a challenge at the Rescue because the doors are always open for the dogs to go in and out. Teresa's solution to this is to buy lots of small electric fan heaters and leave them all over the house set at about 85 degrees, while still leaving the doors open. I constantly turn them down to about 68 and try to explain that dogs don't need to be at 80 degrees, but 5 minutes later they are back at 85 degrees. I hope the neighborhood appreciates us keeping the canyon warm. Our electric bill will be interesting. It's a battle I cannot win. The even more frustrating thing is that every year the heaters from last winter are nowhere to be found and we have to buy new ones. Do the dogs eat them?

Many people have trouble visualizing life at Modjeska Ranch Rescue. The picture below is one corner of the kitchen tonight. I was working in my office when Teresa got home after 13 hours at work, and we chatted for an hour while deciding we were both too tired to eat. The dogs in the kitchen were very relaxed; they like to chill when we are around, preferably within about 6 feet of wherever we are. I still have work to do so Teresa has gone to bed with 6 other dogs while I am back in the office for a while. If you are self-employed, the only thing worse than having a lot to do...is having nothing to do....so I am not complaining as I am busy right now which is a good thing. I believe some people work 8 to 5 and have weekends off? Because I have 2 full time jobs, real estate and rescue, I don't see that happening for me any time soon.

I did enjoy my recent visit to England to see my mom and Family and friends despite it being bittersweet because of family illnesses. We have to make the most of the cards we are dealt! Life is a challenge....it is up to us how we meet the challenge and I choose to do so with a smile on my face even when the picture is not rosy as with my family suffering in England.

My job is to make them smile if it is humanly possible. The dogs in the kitchen agree with me.... I asked them.

Chapter 35

THE "EW" SIDE OF RESCUE OR IS IT RESC—EW?

(Written early 2016)

One of the less glamorous aspects of rescue work, and I am sure one of the least considered by all of you who think of starting a rescue, is the constant need for cleaning up of the food, after it has been through the digestive tract of the animals!

This story comes with a warning for those of you with a sensitive stomach, or if you really do not want to know the horrid story which I will get to later.

Cats are not too bad, as most of them can be trained to use a litter box, although litter-box smell is still one of my least favorite olfactory experiences; horses tend to be easy to deal with depending on how many you have; dogs however, if there are a great number of them, require diligent searching, preferably with good illumination, and careful removal of the post-digestive evidence. The number of dogs at Modjeska Ranch means that it is not unusual for at least one of them to have what we shall call "an upset stomach" for one reason or another! One gets to be quite an expert at interpreting visual health-related clues that are not taught in college. The issue sometimes though is knowing just which dog seems to have semi-liquid or maybe bright yellow poop. Occasionally, if they have eaten a toy, it may even be bright red or blue! By the way, I always do the poop-pickup before I eat breakfast, not afterwards!

We get up early in the morning to address all the animal feeding and medication needs, and one of my jobs is the "pick-up". In the winter, it is not totally light, although I do wait until there is some break in the darkness. Dogs can leave their gifts in the darndest of places and I make sure I am not wearing good shoes, as a hosing is sometimes required before going back in the house and my favorite Italian boots are not hose-able. I am glad to say that most of our dogs usually know to at least "go" outside, except for those that are very old or with medical issues. Carpet in our house is not an option, the whole downstairs is ceramic tile which gets washed with bleach often.

Well, on to the main feature!

We have a large upstairs patio, over my office and the garage. It is probably 30 feet long and 20 feet wide offering plenty of space. Some of the older dogs' sleep in our bedroom, but of course, being older, they still have night-time needs which is why we leave the patio door open and allow them to utilize the patio. One of my morning jobs is to clean off the patio where we keep a large Rubbermaid trash can lined with a heavy black plastic yard bag to collect the night-time poop which is scooped up every morning with a standard poop scooper. The system has worked very efficiently for years.

However, a few weeks ago, there was a sudden windstorm and a downpour of rain which happened while I was away to visit my mother in England and attend my Aunt's funeral. Teresa was coping with the Rescue duties on her own, although Nikki came home for the weekend to help out. Well, the wind managed to blow the top off the large 33-gallon Rubbermaid trashcan, which was half full of dog poop, and which then of course filled up with rainwater. As you can imagine, the resulting "stew" was not very pleasant especially since the wind had folded over part of the black yard bag and there was just a big mess.

On my return from England, and discovering this, I decided that my first job would have to be removing the plastic bag and its contents. I could not risk carrying the bag through the house and tripping even if there was a way to get the bag out in one piece. My plan was to find a way to move/pour/shake everything carefully into new large black yard bags, maybe in three or four "loads" then drag each of them to the front of the house (it was far too heavy to lift). At the front of the patio over the garage door there is a railing fence, and I intended to drop each full bag between the railings and into the large green wheely-bin trash can that I had carefully positioned below.

I managed the first step, getting most of the horrible 30-gallon messy poop-stew into new bags, not perfectly, but a decent job...not too much "spillage". I got the bags to the railings, and the wheely trash bin was in position about 10 feet below.

I worked the first full bag gently between the wooden railings and positioned it directly above the trash can...and let go.

Those of you who know the Rescue will remember that we had to replace the header above our garage door a while ago and at the time of this incident I had not replaced the garage door or the stucco around the door. In the interim we had put a large blue tarpaulin over the garage entrance, and it was hooked onto a series of nails knocked into that surrounding wood-work. This temporary covering had worked well.

However, my face fell, and my stomach turned over, when the black bag full of rainwater/poop mixture caught on one of the nails....and ripped open! I have no idea how it managed to explode in every possible direction, and mostly upwards, but it did, covering me head to toe in this fermented soup of digestive juices. I will have to ask Newton why his laws of gravita-tion allowed me to get "pooped". I admit to standing there for a few minutes wondering what to do. I couldn't put my head in my hands of course as both were covered in poop-soup. My head, hands, clothes, shoes were all dripping in soupy poop and the only way off the patio is back through the house. The garage and the driveway were a mess.

It took a couple of hours to clean me, the patio and the driveway with bleach although the odor seemed to linger long after the cleaning routine.

I hope this story has not passed your "Ew!" threshold and has taught you what not to do in similar circumstances.

Rescue life is such daily fun!

Polo

One day we received a call from the Orange County Polo Club. One of their members had died and left these three furry friends behind. We took them in and found them new homes. We even attended a Polo match as a fundraiser which we had never done before. The Polo Club has since bought land in the canyons. (*not using me as Realtor I'm afraid. I do try to explain to Rescue supporters that using me as their Realtor helps me support the Rescue and many do, so thank you to them, but many more do not, or forget, which is sometimes disappointing*).

The Polo Club bought the land and an old run-down stable and completely redeveloped it. We have not been there, but it looks very impressive when you drive by. They look to have done a great job.

Chapter 36

DON'T JUDGE A BOOK BY ITS COVER

Teresa came home from work one night after 11 and a half hours, on a Sunday! She took in four dogs while she was at work and brought them home to the Rescue!! Two of them are very old and came from the same place.

You may not know this but there is an informal network out there which tries to save old dogs that are on death row at shelters. It's almost a canine underground-railroad made up of caring people who connect with, or transport, or "pull" dogs from shelters.

There are always too many dogs at shelters to rescue them all, and we are but one quite small rescue in Orange County, so I wonder sometimes how we get pleas from people in far off shelters to take dogs that are due to meet their maker. We have taken animals from Lancaster, Palm Desert and Chula Vista at times, all of which are over 100 miles away.

Today, Teresa had agreed with one of these network contacts to take a couple of very old dogs that were at a shelter near Lancaster about 3 hours away! Again "Surely there is someone closer!"

The "railroad" organizes pulling the dogs from the shelter and transporting them to whomever has agreed to take them.

So, back to today, Teresa was at work, and in walked two heavily tattooed, slightly dangerous-looking guys. They asked for Teresa!!!!

Teresa took the dogs in and the guys start crying! These guys, who shall remain nameless, are part of the canine underground-railroad and provide transport saving animals all over the state. They were so happy that Modjeska Ranch was saving these two dogs, with whom they had established a bond, that they were overcome with emotion.

So next time you see some dangerous-looking tattooed guys, remember that they may just be dog rescuers, so don't pre-judge.

Chapter 37

PIG FOOD AND LIZARDS

Why would feeding the pigs at Modjeska Ranch Rescue get the dogs excited and confused, apart from the fact that most dogs just like food of any description?

Well, the pigs have an enclosure which is next to one of the dog areas. In that dog area is a shed. Inside that shed are a couple of large Rubbermaid containers which we fill with the food we give the pigs.

One issue is that the shed in the dog area is only accessible through the house, or over the fence. Teresa and I tend to go for lifting the bags of pig food over the fence which is 5 feet high. Teresa has a bad back, so I lift the bags over the fence; but at one point I had just had surgery, so life is not simple. When we pass these pig food bags over the fence and take them to the shed, I can almost hear the dogs saying "Hey that's food. Shouldn't you stop here and feed us? What's with the pig thing and by the way we really like bacon too".

The dogs "shadow" me as I carry the bags to the shed and they know what's going on. The shed itself and the containers are showing their age. We do our best to keep everything covered as volume pet food tends to attract scurrying little beasties that were uninvited. Some of the "beasties" at the Ranch however are more amusing IMHO. Occasionally I will hear a scream when Teresa sees a lizard in the house, or a much higher register scream if she sees a tarantula as I have said earlier.

Living in an Animal Rescue

A tough day at Modjeska Ranch. Mooshoo the French Bulldog looking a bit old and gray here.

Chapter 38

DOGGIE ACCIDENTS AND AN ESCAPEE

Running an animal rescue presents many challenges, often brings great satisfaction, and can also test one's ability to handle frustration without completely losing one's mind. There are times when we are full of energy, and times when we are simply exhausted and cannot handle anything else.

One week Teresa must have been feeling full of energy as we took in 6 new dogs in a couple of days, all for vastly different reasons.

This resulted today in a couple of incidents that I am sure you will find amusing, although I found them far from that at the time.

One of the challenges with new dogs coming to the Rescue is their "bathroom habits" which, despite the owner's usual claims, can be unpredictable. As I said earlier, we have porcelain tile throughout the downstairs of the house which is very practical. However, that doesn't mean I enjoy cleaning up after doggie accidents. Teresa was not home for a couple of days, so I was preparing the dog food in the kitchen at 5.30 a.m. one morning and I see a pool of doggie leakage on the floor. I cleaned it up and got on with what I am doing. I turned round and there is another pool! Now, if we have one new dog, and I know the habits of the older residents, I can pinpoint the culprit. However, when there are multiple new dogs, that is not possible, and it is very frustrating. Is that dog just sniffing around in a curious fashion, or is he preparing to make more work for me? By mid-morning the leakage seems to be under control, but I was not convinced and still had not pinpointed the culprit, I always seemed to be out of sight when it happened. Maybe they were all playing a joke on me, just waiting until I wasn't looking?

When I had finished preparing the dog food, the two bulldogs' food is put outside the door as they are very possessive on everyone's food, so they eat outside in a fenced area near the kitchen, and the others eat inside. I went outside to put down their food, and who is looking at me there by the kitchen fence but a new dog that was supposed to be in a large, fenced area with 3 other dogs on the far side of the house. How did he get there? How did he get out? We haven't had an escapee for years. I said, "Oh dear!", or I may have used more expressive language.

144

I approached the dog slowly saying nice things, and he turned and ran off through the bushes and down the dirt road that runs across the four acres of our property at the back of the house. I gave chase. I am still in decent shape for my age, but I cannot outrun a dog unless it is a very small one. I lost sight of him as he rounded a bend on the dirt road and seemed to go into my neighbor's yard headed for the main road. I hesitated, thinking "Shall I chase him out there, or go back and get the car and go round onto the main road?" I decided to get the car, a leash and some dog biscuits. I drove round onto the main road and hunted up and down for a while but to no effect. We had only had this guy a few days and I doubted he would know his way back. At this point also my thoughts were still interrupted by wondering "How on earth did he get out!?!?"

I drove back home, pulled into the driveway, and there he was! Looking at me as if nothing was wrong! I got out of the car and he shot off up the road again! Argh!! I took the car after him, and he stopped after about a hundred yards. I stopped the car and threw open the driver door. He trotted down to the car and jumped in! What a relief!

I brought him home and put him in a large crate while I investigated how he had got out of the area he was in. The other 3 dogs were all still there so how had this guy managed it?

I finally found that he had forced open just the bottom edge of a vinyl gate and slipped through, so I secured the gate in many parts with wire and rope just to make sure before I put the escapee back.

My bits of wire and rope did not look elegant but did the job. Fixing it so it looks nice could go on that long list of things that never get done. Running the Rescue has made me understand when I see farms that have pieces of equipment lying around seemingly abandoned and rusty, there just are not enough hours in the day.

Back to the story. I took him back out and his doggie friends all seemed pleased to see him and he them.

I went back to feeding everyone else.

5 minutes later, I looked out of the kitchen window and he's out again! I expressed myself using language of which my mother would not approve. Fortunately, I chased him around the garden and managed to corner him at which point he gave up calmly. Back to the crate while I investigate again. He had bitten through the ties I had put on the gate! Smart dog.

I now have a completely new piece of metal fence tied in place which is very ugly, but he is not getting out again! He seems happy and friendly, but he obviously likes to run.

No harm done apart from my blood pressure and my morning schedule. Now it was back to work to sell and buy houses for clients so we can pay for this place and feed everyone!

Modjeska Ranch Rescue Kitchen

When friends come over sometimes they go home with a new friend

Modjeska Ranch kitchen at 5am each day.

We do have another small fridge in the kitchen but sometimes the main fridge is a little full

Chapter 39

WHAT'S IN YOUR CUPBOARD?

Most homes have cupboards in the kitchen and/or bedroom containing medications such as headache tablets, spare bottles of shampoo, soap etc.

We have many cupboards full to overflowing with medications, treatments, brushes, shampoo, tick lotion, perfume and enzymes for removing odors.

However, if I have a headache, can I find an Advil or a Tylenol? If we are out of shampoo in the shower and I am dripping wet searching for a new bottle, can I find one? Sometimes I get out of the shower and go the towel closet and there are no towels. They have been used to clean up floors and dry off dogs. Somehow, even though our closets have doors, I will look for a pair of socks, or shoes, or even sometimes a toothbrush or hairbrush and eventually find it in the yard with holes/toothmarks or just in pieces. My reaction depends on the day. If I am working at home, I may be calm and resigned to this, but if I was getting out of the shower to get dressed to meet a client, and I am running late, I might just let fly with some impolite language.

Chapter 40

MORNING AT MODJESKA

I woke this morning to the sight and sound of gently rustling dead leaves. There are not many dead things that are beautiful but dead leaves have a strange fascination. I remember having to collect leaves in school and press them in books. Leaves are even collected and sold, scented, in bags with ribbons as potpourri. What other dead things attract such fond attention?

The slightly unusual aspect of this morning's leaves display was its location on my bedroom floor. Of course, my house is Modjeska Ranch Rescue, and its function as my family's home is often only an afterthought to its function as a home for a variety of God's other creatures. This usually results in most of the doors in the house remaining open, come wind, rain or shine. Last night the bedroom door was open to the outside as our new arrival, Harry the St Bernard, can't decide whether he wants to lie down inside or outside. The night was quite windy, and this resulted in a number of said dead leaves blowing through the open door and ending up in the bedroom. Maybe I will make a Modjeska Ranch "potpourri" to sell for donations to the Rescue. Mind you, with so many dogs around, I would of course need to check each leaf carefully to make sure its scent only consists of tree-related substances!

My job this morning, as you know by now, is to feed the horses, goats, cows and pigs, replenish water where necessary, and then pick up all the dog poop. I know this is everyone's ideal start to the day, but I must keep the task to myself despite protestations that I am being selfish in doing so.

In January it is sometimes still dark when I begin. In such cases I start with the feeding etc., as picking up dog poop in the dark is hazardous. I leave that to your imagination. The cows are always ready to eat, almost shouting at me as soon as they see movement. The horse/goat contingent, while not refusing food, look at me a little more skeptically...what are you doing up at this time of day? The cows are fed alfalfa hay, and a grain mix called 4-way, which looks a little like a mixture of granola and Quaker oatmeal breakfast. The horse and goats get alfalfa and "sweet-feed" which is a mixture of grains with sweet molasses. The 4-way and the sweet-feed are much more popular than the alfalfa; it's a bit like giving a child dry cornflakes and ice-cream. The only thing the horses/goats love more is carrots. Isn't it strange that the lowly carrot, which is not a wildly popular vegetable with humans, is a delicacy to a horse or a goat?

While I am doing this, Teresa is feeding and medicating the dogs and cats with insulin, eye medication, pain relief etc., and getting ready for work at the Vet office.

Once I have completed the animal duties, I must eat breakfast. I cannot function without breakfast. Teresa doesn't eat breakfast no matter how much I insist it's the most important meal of the day and I believe the most enjoyable. I'd rather have a good breakfast than a meal at the best restaurant in town. My breakfast must be English tea, dry cereal and multigrain toast. The day is simply not going to be right if I miss it. The tea of choice at the moment is Taylor's Yorkshire Gold. Teresa prefers Liptons although is starting to drink Oolong. Liptons all-purpose bags, in my humble opinion, are not really tea, despite Liptons being an old-established brand in England. To my taste, Liptons is to tea what Bud light is to beer! (that may start an argument!)

Breakfast is accompanied by a quick check on world news from the BBC and various podcasts on my Ipad. I believe knowing what is going on, and why, in different countries and cultures is the only way to gain a rational view of what happens there and also here. Perspective is everything. Lack of knowledge about how things really work elsewhere, in my opinion, reduces one's opinions to mere unfounded, ill-informed assertions on some major issues. We are all entitled to an opinion, but the value of that opinion depends on how well-informed and thoughtful it is.

Back to the story, after breakfast then it's time for a shower. However, I often take five minutes to ruffle dog heads and play with them a little, and sometimes take pictures when everyone seems calm. The light is good for pictures in the morning. Taking good pictures of lots of dogs is very difficult. One of them is always moving just when you have a good shot, or they want to come to you just as you "click", giving you a close- up of a nose that looks very long. Posing for photographs is not a natural doggie trait. Each good picture I get is usually the result of 30 or 40 pictures taken. If it's a picture we really need, then of course the dog will never cooperate! Teresa often asks me "Can you just get a "good" picture of ****". She wants it in 5 minutes. It doesn't work like that.

So, shower time, hoping that there are towels in the closet that have not been used for dogs to lie on or at least not recently. Then dressing is not a problem, I got the hang of that when I was young, but getting out of the house in business clothes, without slobber and lick stains and dog hair is a talent I am still working on. Suggestions welcome but getting dressed in the driveway is a little extreme. Having said that, Teresa has done that on occasion when we have been going out somewhere special.

As I climb into my car, the cows are usually "mooing" loudly, indicating that they have finished their food and, as far as they are concerned, it is time for more.

There are days when this routine is slightly magical in that we all like to have a purpose in life and like to think we are contributing in some way. However, I have to admit there are days when my mindset is not quite so "enlightened" and I wonder what it's like to wake up to a normal household!

By the way, before I go to work today, I must patch up my hand; when feeding the horses and goats I slipped on the rubber mats on a slope and smashed my hand against the corral. I got no sympathy from the goats at all!

Chapter 41

PEBBLES

Today Pebbles died. Just lay down and expired.

She was a waggy-backside boxer/bulldog mix with a back-story that tears at the heart but also gets one frustrated about that other type of creature, people.

Pebbles came to us from a humane society where they know us well, or at least know Teresa well. Pebbles was picked up after a police raid on a house had found her, fully grown but only about 20lbs weight, with skin hanging off her skeleton like an old, wrinkled sweater. When she was examined, her stomach contained only small stone pebbles, having presumably eaten them for want of anything else. The police found another dog starved to death in the backyard of the house. A word of warning to those who abuse animals, this guy went to jail. Damn right too!

Pebbles was taken to the humane society who then called and asked if we would take Pebbles and try to get her healthy. 3 months later she weighed a solid 50 lbs and was a funny affectionate playmate for us and all the other dogs, although a bit slobbery...which as I have said is not good if you are wearing khaki pants and hoping to look quasi professional.

A couple of years later the Humane Society opened a new building. Teresa and Pebbles were invited to the opening as special guests.

Teresa and Pebbles from many years ago

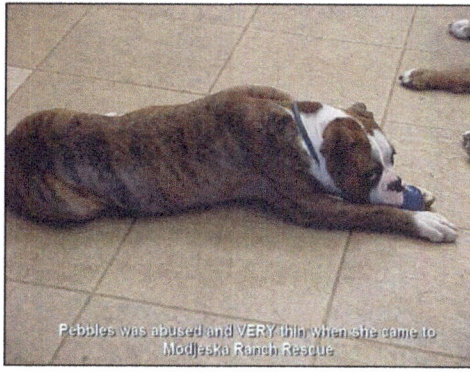

Pebbles was abused and VERY thin when she came to Modjeska Ranch Rescue

Chapter 42

GOODBYE ROSES!

When we bought the house that has become Modjeska Ranch Rescue or borrowed it from the bank may be more accurate, the front of the house was bordered by ten stunning rose trees about 4 feet high.

They bloomed repeatedly during the year, in a variety of bright colors, red, yellow, peach and some a mixture of these colors. It was hard to keep up with the "dead-heading" because they seemed to bloom all the time.

Gradually, the number of rose trees has diminished, until this weekend the number arrived at zero. Very sad.

This is not due to any horticultural Tsunami. When you have as many dogs as we do, and the individuals in the population change regularly, there are always one or two who like to dig, and rose tree roots must have some special taste, unless there are burrowing animals around the roots for which the dogs are searching. Lucy finally decided to dig the roots of the last remaining rose tree. The house looks a little bare now.

The other side of the house still has a few nice rose trees I am glad to say so we have some color, and we have lots of orange trees that give huge numbers of oranges and very fragrant orange blossom and a citron tree that produces bags-full of citrons that have very thick knobbly skin, not much juice and are apparently the granddaddy of lemons.

Talking of roses, roses like clay and we are on almost pure clay here where the water percolates very slowly. Roses also like horse manure of which we have ample supplies.

When I was young, we had lots of roses in my parent's garden in England. Horse manure however was not common in the city where we lived. That made the rounds of the "Rag and Bone" man an event which carried more import than you may initially imagine.

Most of you in the US are probably thinking the "Rag and Bone" man is from an episode on Law and Order or a Stephen King movie or someone from the very up-market menswear store in New York, started by 2 British guys. It is no such thing.

A rag and bone man were someone who went around neighborhoods, often with a horse and cart, and collected old rags, unwanted clothes and other items, which he then sold later to merchants. He was sort of a travelling thrift shop collector. Sometimes he would give out something in return, like goldfish for children. He would drive his cart down the road shouting the kind of unintelligible words that we used to hear from newspaper street sellers. "Raaanbone"…"Raanbone" as opposed to some garbled version of the newspaper's name. I sort of miss those newspaper cries.

The rag and bone man's horse was important. The point is that the horse in front of the cart would on occasion give in to the needs of nature. Neighbors with otherwise rather middle-class lifestyles would run into the street and scoop up the valuable horse manure to take back for their rose trees or more often send their children to do this strange duty. I can't imagine children in our Orange County CA "bubble" running into the street to pick up horse poop as it might spoil their Gucci loafers or $150 basketball shoes.

So, I will have to plant some new roses…and introduce the dogs to the delights of the smell of flowers rather than the taste! Having said that I have a wife who does not like roses, so she really doesn't see the tragedy the same way I do.

Chapter 43

THE DARK AND WINDY CANYON

I arrived home in the dark. It was about 7.30 and I heard by text that the wind had been howling in Modjeska. Only 15 minutes away in what was then my office in Rancho Santa Margarita all had seemed calm, save a few more people interested about the dangers or opportunities of the Real Estate market in these turbulent times. I used again that useful expression which explains that my job is to navigate the storm, but I cannot calm the ocean.

Pulling into the driveway, not a breath of wind disturbed my hair as I emerged from the car, even though I badly need a haircut. A few of the 25 dogs greeted me from the other side of the house or the upstairs balcony, and the horses blew through their fascinatingly loose lips as if to say, "About time, we are hungry"? I could hear this as the night was still and the stars twinkled in a Peter-Pan-clear sky.

Modjeska Canyon is a magical place on a night like this. I just stood and listened for a moment. Life is about moments. My troubles faded away just for that moment.

I dropped my Vons Grocery bag in the kitchen, which I admit contained a bottle of wine for a hopefully relaxed Friday evening at home. By the way, "relaxed" and "home" are relative terms when you live in an animal rescue. Living with over 20 dogs in the house, some cats, 5 horses, 3 goats and 7 pigs, is "busy", that's a good word to use, especially when both of you also work full time or more.

Anyway, I had been expecting carnage from the wind. In the past, large trees have been blown down, roofs from corrals have landed in the street, hay has been tumbled down the hill, and animals have gone crazy.

So, in the calm of this beautiful evening, I quickly changed from my good clothes into something more animal-friendly and went to feed and water the horses and other "external" animals.

Ahhhh! It really had been windy.

The tarps, weighted down with stones, had been blown away, the buckets of heavy feed had been blown over, the buckets of tack and tools had been spread around a large area, which I had to search with a flashlight.

The horses and goats, probably having forgotten the wind, were all looking at me as if I was a lunatic........forget that stuff and feed us!!

Halfway through clearing up the mess the wind started again, out of nowhere! Having fed the hungry ones, I covered everything and weighted it down as best I could and made sure it was rain proofed. We don't get a lot of rain and wind in the canyons, maybe 5 or 6 days a year, but when it comes, it is violent.

So now I am writing this having fed the animals, eaten my own dinner, and somehow the wine has also disappeared. Funny that!!!!

Can we come in your office and play with the paper ??

If I don't close the door to my office

So honey, that big sale at Bloomingdales has cat beds with real fish sown into the fabric.

Chapter 44

TOWELS

An animal rescue has need for large supplies of things that may not immediately come to mind. In fact, if they do, the reason for them may make one wish to divert one's thoughts to something else. The consequences of shortages produce unforeseen situations, and one of those occurred the other day.

I am talking of towels. At a rescue, towels have many uses; they are warm for dogs to lay on if the tile is cold, they help to mop up "accidents", they help to dry dogs who have been washed, they can be put on chairs and couches as extra comfort or to protect something, they can be used to wrap a dog and keep it still while attending to ear cleaning or administering medication, etc etc. There are, of course, a number of uses to which we put towels that render them unfit for repeat usage, but I will leave the picture of animals with sudden, severe, and repeated "digestive" problems for you to imagine.

As most of you know by now, at Modjeska Ranch Rescue, the separation between "dog space" and "human space" does not exist. The dogs and cats, separately, live with us in the house. The same principle applies in a way to towels. If towels are needed for animal use, they are normally grabbed from the nearest closet, which often means that our own human towels are "re-categorized" at very short notice, irrespective of how soft, luxurious and expensive they may be.

We are lucky that many supporters donate old towels so our supply of towels for the dogs is usually good and finding cupboard space for them is sometimes more the issue. Well, this was obviously not the case just recently. I was preparing to jump into the shower before heading for work as showering is always a good thing after the morning feeding routine. I opened the towel cupboard to grab a towel. Well, the cupboard was bare. I pulled on some shorts and went downstairs to the laundry room, assuming that it must have a LOT of towels both clean and waiting for the washing machine but not a towel in sight! Puzzling! I confess it was a good thing that I was alone in the house as I utilized my full vocabulary wondering where the towels had gone! I was running around saying "My word, we seem to be out of towels!", or I may have used other more colorful words to that effect.

Anyway, I did take a shower and improvised myself dry, still wondering just where all those towels had gone. I wish I could shake myself dry like a dog!

Rescue life has other challenges that may be even more horrifying than the idea of me wet and naked hunting for a towel. Recently we took in an old miniature pincher. Not the most huggable character we have ever had, but he's old and not too well, so we'll forgive him his moodiness and irritability. Well, he is semi house-trained so usually will "go" outside with a little encouragement. That's the good part. The "eeew" part is that the part of his anatomy which identifies him as a male performs fine when he needs to "go" but does not retract again into its protective "housing". In order for him not to have infection and cleanliness problems, this process must be assisted manually by one of us. Volunteers for this job should email immediately.

Peanuts

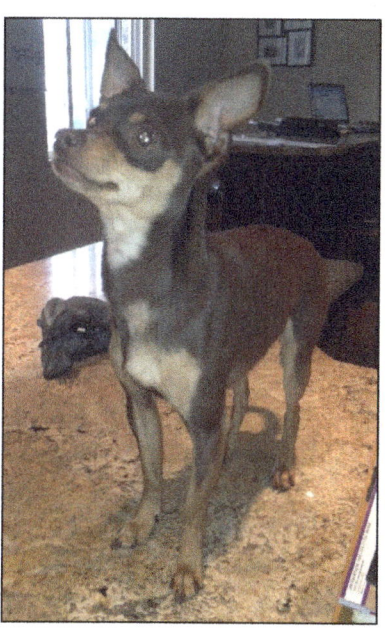

Peanuts the young "MinPin" was adopted to a great family. He was a fun little guy. His previous family had been forced to move out of their home and into a small apartment with their children and were very upset to give up Peanuts.

We had him for a couple of months and were very surprised that he did not get adopted much sooner. Peanuts loved to be picked up and carried around but wriggled constantly; it was like carrying a chicken, if you've ever had that dubious pleasure.

Ruining Clothes

About this time, it was getting warmer at the ranch. It seemed to have been a long and wet winter. The wet weather gives us special challenges, and ruins lots of shoes and clothes which get covered in the wet red clay on those occasions when I am too lazy to get changed before doing the corral chores in the evening. I admit sometimes to wanting to get the chores done when I get home and not taking the time to change. I can't tell you how many pairs of khakis I have with pale bleach splotches below the knees from mopping the floors in my work clothes, and even on shirts from when I have changed the mop bucket water. If it's a shirt I really like, then I do get a little angry, but I have only myself to blame.

Goldie

Goldie the old Icelandic Pony is losing her winter coat in this picture. She is changing from a long-silky-haired beauty to a horse with a normal coat. There is hair EVERYWHERE. I am sure we could make a Marylin Monroe wig from Goldie's hair.

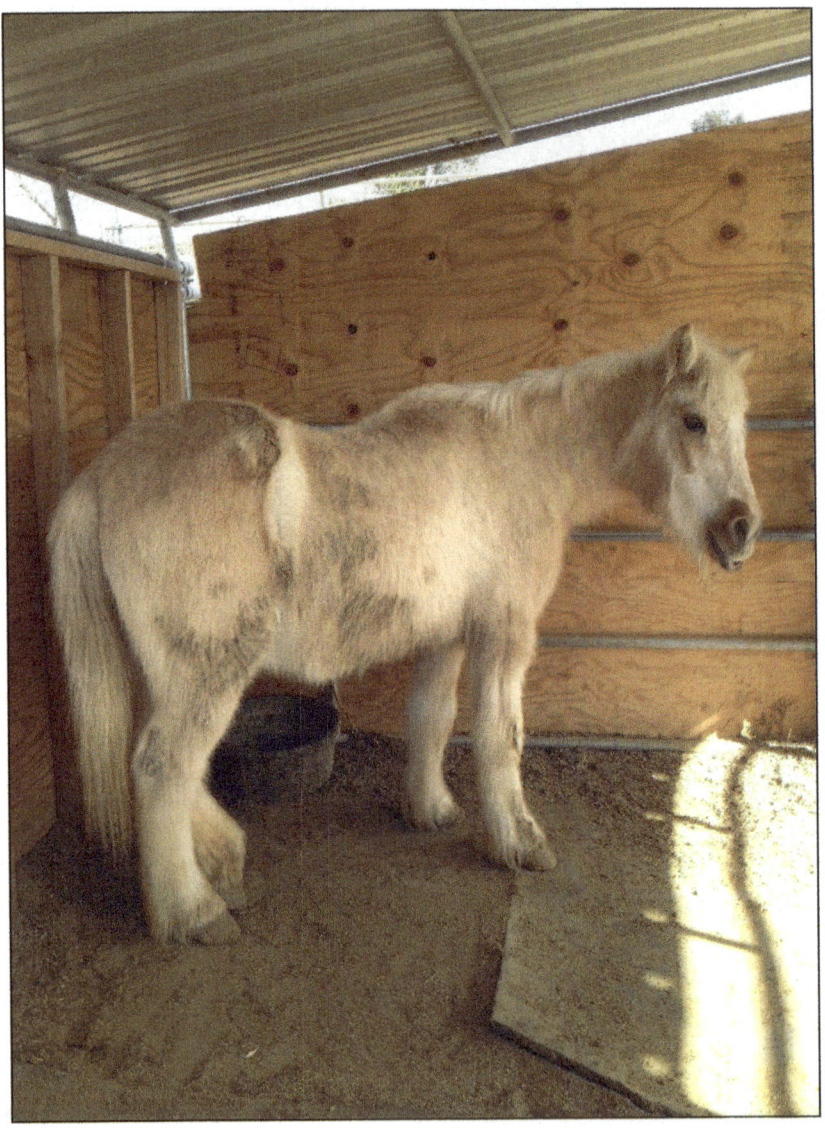

Chapter 45

RITZI

A few years ago, we took in a horse that was so neglected that he looked like a skeleton with a dirty sheet of skin thrown over him. His name was Ritzi, a Morgan, and we were not sure if he could survive. It took about 6 months to get him in great shape, by which time he was a very handsome horse. A lucky adopter got themselves a beauty for free. Believe it or not, these pictures of Ritzi are of the same horse, the first two when he arrived and the last one when he left to his new home. Good food, Vet care and TLC can go a long way.

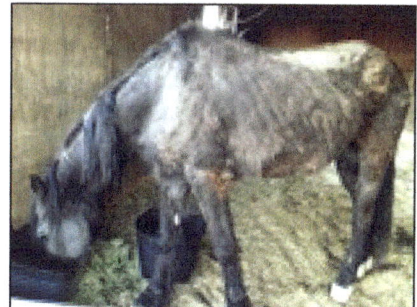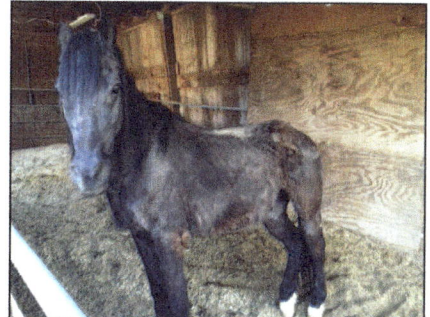

BEFORE

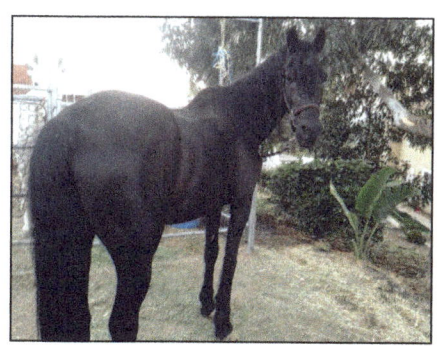

AFTER

Chapter 46

LORD OF THE RING

A few years after Teresa and I got married, I was doing my morning chores, feeding the horses in the corral. It was about the time that we had rescued 14 horses from the track and from their destiny at a slaughterhouse or a PMU farm, more about PMU farms later. The horses were wandering the pasture while I tried to fling hay around so they could all get some. The ground was soft and muddy after one of our rare rainstorms. The Rescue property is on a hill that leads into Modjeska Canyon and the hill is clay, almost solid clay, which can be horribly muddy in the wet, and as solid as concrete in the summer with fine red dust blowing around if it is hot and windy. For those of you who only see horses in pictures and never get close up to one, horses are very large and very heavy, so heavy horses on wet clay creates a mud which doesn't seem to bother the horses at all but does suck your boots off when you try to walk through it.

Well, I flung a leaf of hay out into the corral to get it far away and my wedding ring flew off into the mud. It had been a touch loose but my knuckle and the base of my ring finger are about the same size so I can't make it any tighter. I thought I saw just where it went, so I waded into the mud and poked around....and poked around...and poked around. I could not find it. Never did find it.

I spent about 12 years not wearing a wedding ring. Occasionally Teresa would mention that I should get one. Must have been the hundreds of Rescue groupies she was concerned about; you know how wellies and mud and the smell of horse/dog poop is a really effective chick magnet!

So last year Teresa had mentioned it again. We have a friend, and a real estate client of mine, who owns a jewelry store, so I went to see him, and he showed me some options. While I was thinking about it, fate took a hand. I was sorting through some of my mother's things, she had passed away a couple of years earlier, and I came across her wedding ring. She had tiny fingers so it would not fit me, but I took it to our friend the jeweler, and he managed to expand it by adding extra gold and then worked it to fit me. Problem solved and with a ring that still had great significance.

After a few months, the ring split. It was 70 years old and had worn thin. My friend the jeweler fixed it again but warned that this may keep happening; the only long-term solution would be to form a new ring inside it, which would be expensive. I said I would think about that if it split again.

A few weeks later, we were hit with the Corona Virus pandemic. The early lockdown was sort of partial. I was working from home but still had to go out occasionally to pick up things. Well, I went to my car and started it, I looked down and my heart sank as I thought "Where is my ring?"

Teresa and I searched, and then she searched more as I had to be somewhere. No luck.

Teresa had a good thought. She had taken a picture of me the night before, wrapped up in boots and coat to feed the horses and goats in the rain, and she could see my ring in the picture, so we knew it had to be on the property. We searched again, no luck, and eventually concluded it must be in the corral from when I was shoveling horse poop that morning, again in the rain, so my hands were very slippery.

We considered getting a metal detector. A neighbor has one so we thought we would do that once it stopped raining. Maybe we would even find the first one too!

Teresa went upstairs to have a shower leaving me to cook dinner that night. When she came down she said "If you could have anything in the world right now what would it be?" I was puzzled and tempted to make some crass humorous remark about romantic assignations with Julia Roberts (my default behavior is humor).

Suddenly I saw my ring on her finger. It had been wrapped in a towel that I had showered with the day before and was in the laundry basket.

Now I do NOT wear my ring to the corral, or if I am going to be flinging anything. I am very pleased I have it back. Teresa put it on my finger again.

This is my gear for when I feed the corral animals on a cold rainy night. Sexy huh? I wear it so rarely that it takes me a while to find it.

You can see here the effect of rain on clay. There is a covered stall area where I am standing to take this picture and about an acre fenced beyond these two horses, but sudden rain can make a mess really fast. Inside the covered area we spread around bales and bales of "shavings" which help to dry the area and give the animals something nice and soft to hang around in. This picture is of two of the racehorses we saved from the slaughterhouse in 2009.

Chapter 47

PIXIE

This chapter was written by Teresa.

It's a Friday night and for a change my husband asked me to meet him at a local pub for dinner. I usually always say "No" as I want to get home to all the critters, but this time I said I would see him there at 6.30. I arrived and we got a table and ordered food. Russ looked at me and said, "I'm not sure if we can help but read this text I received today".

I started reading and tears were in my eyes. The text was asking for help on a 3-year-old French Bulldog with paralyzed back legs. The owner said she had called over 20 rescues and was told to euthanize. After I finished reading this, I looked at Russ and said "I need to call her; be back in a few minutes". I stepped outside and wondered what I could do for this girl. I called the number and the voice of a sad woman said hello.

I introduced myself and explained about our rescue and asked her to tell me about the Frenchie.

She started out telling me she has 3 young sons and her husband had just passed away. On top of that she has a medical condition which means she cannot walk and get around properly. She and the boys had moved to Orange County to be close to schools to which they could walk or take the Metro Bus, as she cannot drive.

When they moved into their rental, the Frenchie, "Pixie", jumped off the couch and somehow hurt her back so now she could not move her back half at all. She had taken Pixie to a Vet who had charged her a lot of money to tell her that Pixie would need over $5,000 of surgery. She told them she could not afford that. The response was that her alternative was to euthanize. She said she could not make that decision and would have to talk to her sons as they love Pixie. The Vet showed her how to express Pixie's bladder as she could not do it on her own and said it should be done 2 or 3 times a day. The Mom took Pixie home and the boys said they would help until they could find someone with a better answer for Pixie.

The boys started going to school late, or not at all, as they knew Mom could not cope with Pixie's bladder needs during the day.

After hearing this story, I decided we would take Pixie to Modjeska Ranch Rescue and see what we could do to give her a future. I told the mom that I would call her back when I could make arrangements to pick her up.

The next Monday morning, there was a wildfire at Irvine Lake quite close to our house and we were on put on high alert. We had 30 dogs, 98 cats, 5 goats, 2 mini-horses, fish and even a hermit crab, so we have to have a game plan for evacuation if that became necessary. I called Pixie's Mom to explain and she said, "Please come no later than Wednesday!". I wasn't sure why she was so anxious, but I told her I would be there between 7-8am Wednesday.

We were lucky with the fire as the wind went North and West rather than South to us, so on Wednesday I headed to pick up Pixie

Having worked at a Vet office for 15 years and having run a rescue since 2001, I knew I had to stay strong not just for the pet but also for the family.

I knocked on the door at 7.50 am. One of the sons opened the door and let me in. "Mom" introduced me to her sons who were staying strong for her. Inside an X-pen in the living room was Miss Pixie who was trying to drag herself around to get some attention. The Mother explained that the boys were missing school to help her with Pixie, and the school had called to say they cannot have any more absences unless they are sick, and this was causing Mom a lot of stress. My eyes teared up. This was the reason I had to be there early as the boys must be at school by 9am. The two youngest ones walked to a nearby school and the eldest took a Metro bus or a ride from a friend.

As they were all saying good-bye and giving me Pixie's things, the pain and the sadness of the family tore me up and I cried for the 20-minute drive home.

Pulling in our driveway I wasn't sure how this was going to work, especially when we have several other dogs with special medical needs. Miss Pixie met everyone and wanted to get down and play. Pixie didn't know she couldn't play. I put Pixie in our bedroom with the bathroom door open but closed in with a baby gate. She loved her bed and nice comforter. Pixie wasn't sure what her new place would bring her. I started researching about French Bulldogs and the paralysis issue. We have one other Frenchie here called Mushu (although Russ spells it Mooshoo, who knows?) Mushu has not had any issues but is getting old. After a couple of hours reading, it becomes clear that Frenchies can have back issues. It seems that sometimes a cart is a great answer, but I know a cart would not work here at our home as we have so many dogs, they would knock her over. The articles I read talked about surgeries, the cost of them and further treatments.

As I was processing all this information, I remembered that I worked with and knew well an amazing Vet who does acupuncture, Dr Hsu. She was working in Irvine.

I wrote Dr Hsu a long email with all the information to see what she would say. I was searching for the right way to proceed on Pixie's health. I then took care of all the feeding and cleaning up, and Pixie seemed to be sleeping and adjusting better than I thought she would.

The next morning there was a message on my phone and an email asking me to make an appointment to see Dr Hsu. I called and made the earliest appointment I could, which was the next day. Now my next thought was how was this going to be paid for, as we have several seniors with medical issues. However, I knew we would find a way. As they say "It takes a Village" to help run our Rescue and we have been blessed with support from so many people from the local canyons to Canada. We are so thankful.

The next day, I put Pixie in a secure crate in my old Honda Pilot and took her to see Dr Hsu, hoping for the best.

We pulled into the parking lot and I carried Pixie inside. The receptionist was nice, and I filled out all the paperwork. Pixie sat by my legs wanting to see what was next.

When we were put in a treatment- room and I saw Dr Hsu, I felt a huge weight off my shoulders. She examined Pixie and told me she had seen several French Bulldogs with this issue. She explained that she wanted to start acupuncture today and will see from the next couple of these treatments just what could be done. Pixie wasn't sure about all the little needles and the electro-vibes going into her, but she did well for about 45 minutes when the needles were pulled out.

Dr Hsu told me to make another appointment for the next week and to keep Pixie confined and to be sure to help her release her bladder. Leaving the Vet office, I felt Pixie's family would be glad to hear the news, but I decided not to tell them yet and get their hopes up.

The second visit went smoothly and after an hour we were ready to head home for some chicken and rice and a new soft bed for Pixie. The next morning, I saw a wet potty pad and I saw Pixie trying to stand and walk to the gate; she was still weak but didn't show it. Wow! I texted Dr Hsu and she was very happy but said we must take baby steps.

By the 3rd visit Pixie was now starting to walk and be able to urinate on her own. We thought this was amazing.

Dr Hsu explained that more therapy would help but will never make her perfect. We discussed surgery but both agreed the therapy was working and there was no guarantee that surgery would give a better result.

Dr Hsu sent home some "meds" for her to give twice a day with Glucosamine.

Every day we saw more improvement; if she fell or slipped, she would just pick herself back up, and she enjoyed being able to hang with her new doggie friends for a while.

My heart was hurting for the three boys and the mom as they loved Pixie, and I was now planning that this could be a great Christmas present for them if Pixie could go back home. I talked it over with Dr Hsu and our Rescue Board. They all agreed it would be great. We knew they couldn't afford to take care of medical issues, so we decided to cover Pixie's expenses. This made me feel good and would put some smiles on a family's faces. We had six weeks before Christmas, so the planning started.

Firstly, I wanted to talk to Pixie's Mom and tell her the game plan. I tried to call her but didn't get an answer so I wrote her a letter telling her we would like her and the boys to have an early Christmas and that we were willing to return Pixie and cover medical treatments by our Vet for Pixie's lifetime. We had never done this before.

I received her reply. She said the boys would be thrilled but she had to think about what was best for Pixie. They have steps to the upstairs and Pixie would try to climb them which she can't do, and one accident could be a disaster. I tried to hold back my tears as she explained that with her own medical issues, she can't move around too much in the house and who would take Pixie outside, and if Pixie became paralyzed again, then the boys would be sad again as they had just lost their Dad and Pixie. As a Mom I felt her pain; she was having to be both parents and trying hard to keep her family happy and she was in pain with her own medical condition and the loss of her husband. She had maxed out her credit cards on their other French Bulldog. She told me she would think about it and text me later in the week.

Pixie by this time was a wobbly girl but got around rather well and was put in an area of her own if she got too active with the other dogs.

I kept thinking about Pixie's family and I understood what the mom was saying. Three weeks went by, and I didn't hear from her. I sent her an email and asked if she had thought any more about the Christmas plan. I told Pixie's story to several of our friends, and they all wanted to help in any way they could.

Pixie at Modjeska Ranch Rescue with her friend Lucy

Two days later Pixie's Mom called me and said she herself will be needing surgery and even though she loves Pixie, and the boys miss her, that Pixie is better off at Modjeska Ranch. She said sometimes you have to think about the future and it's best for Pixie that way. Tears were running down my face. As a mom, and also as a Mom to all our critters, I understood.

So I decided to give the family Christmas gifts from Pixie. There were gifts not just from us, but from other supporters of our rescue also, which made this very special. The boys would enjoy gift cards to buy themselves something and Pixie's Mom had some presents too. This is what Christmas is for, giving and being thankful.

Two days before Christmas, I knocked on the door and handed Pixie's Mom a bag of gifts from Pixie. She thanked me and told me she wasn't feeling well. I wished her a Merry Christmas and a great New Year.

Leaving the neighborhood, I realized that Pixie will be ours now and she will have what she will always need. I came home and held her and cried, but I wasn't sad because I knew this was another learning experience in life.

Christmas came and Pixie, like the other 30 dogs, got their special Holiday meal and new beds and blankets which were being dropped off by nice supporters and Amazon boxes were arriving every day. All the critters were very happy with all the presents.

Well, it was soon time to take Pixie back to Dr Hsu to get acupuncture and learn the game plan for 2018.

I made the appointment for January 29th, and I chuckled thinking I should stop giving her so many treats. The holidays are over, and we have to keep her slimmed down so there is less pressure on her back. As a new year begins, a new journey starts for this girl. There will be challenges, but as I tell everyone we all have special needs and we will work hard to make her life enjoyable, and we will be her family forever. Dr Hsu came into the room, and we went over Pixie's progress and her future journey.

There will be more acupuncture and a refill on her meds to help with the muscles.

Pixie knows the routine now, so Dr Hsu puts all the needles in one by one in the spots where Pixie needs the most treatment. It lasts 45 minutes and Pixie is always ready to get out of there. It is obvious that the treatment makes Pixie feel much better. When I put her in the car, she looked at me and I could almost hear her say "Thank you".

It only took 30 minutes to get home and as soon as Pixie saw her friends, she was ready to play and enjoy herself. To Pixie it's just another day at Modjeska Ranch Rescue.

Pixie will never forget her first family and she enjoyed being with them. Now she will feel the love at the Rescue with all her new furry friends.

Pixie with her friends on the couch

Pixie can't decide whether to drink or jump in on a hot day

Nothing like a little French ass to lay your head on

Chapter 48

BATMAN AND ROBIN FIND A NEW HOME

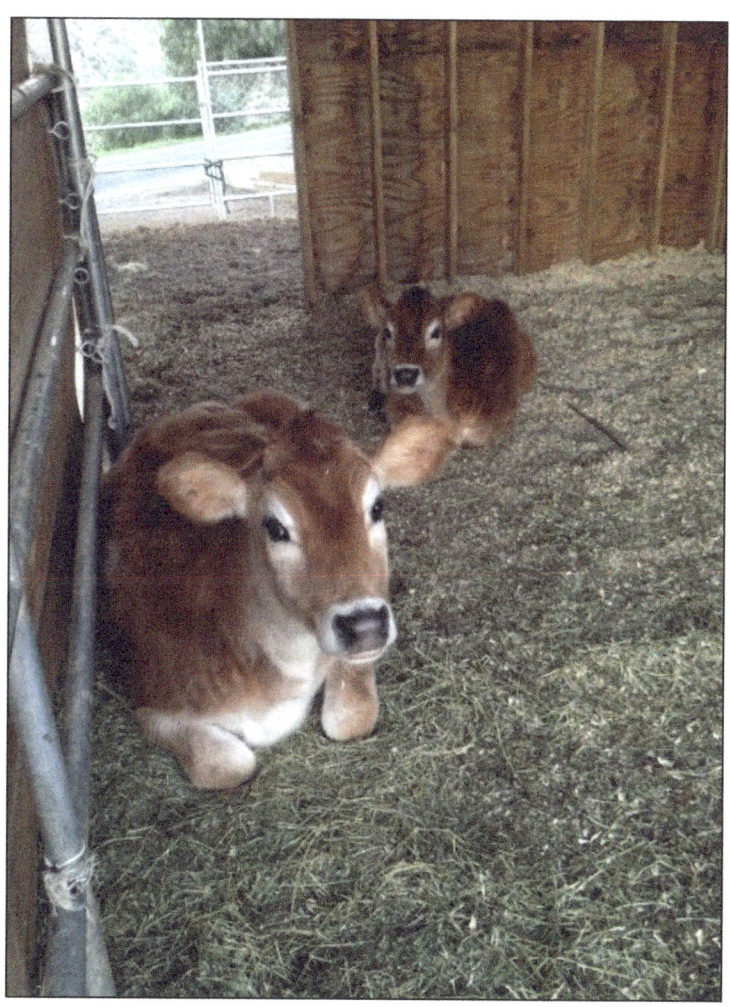

Every year there is a large County Fair in Orange County. Appropriately it is held at "The Fairgrounds". Part of the Fair consists of booths selling all manner of things, and strange foods like deep fried ice cream, deep fried

Oreo cookies, frozen coffee on a stick, and fried turkey legs on a stick If they can fry it, you can buy it.

There is also a farm section, where you can wander through pens of farm animals and watch animal displays and competitions. Cows, sheep, goats, horses, rabbits, tortoises, birds etc, you get the picture.

One year, a friend and supporter of ours attended the Fair and while they were wandering around the farm area, they were enamored of two beautiful 3-month-old Swiss cows. They were so small and fine-featured they almost looked like deer. On taking up discussion with the attendants of the farm, she was horrified to learn that their fate after the Fair involved being turned into veal. So, she bought them! And had them delivered to Modjeska Ranch. We had not had cows before, so a new experience awaited.

Well, firstly, what cows do a lot is eat. They eat as much as you can give them. We took advice on what to feed them and it was mostly "3 way" grain mix with occasional other treats.

We named them Batman and Robin, one being somewhat larger than the other, and they grew amazingly quickly. The cute little deer-like appearance was soon replaced by a large cow, a very large cow. Large cows process their food and then leave large plops of "dung". Oh dung SMELLS! Having had a lot of animals, we have never had that problem before. Even though the cows were in a corral, if the wind was in the right direction, we could smell the cows. It's much worse than horses or goats or pigs, none of which have treated us to such olfactory experiences.

Another thing is that cows can be quite moody and boisterous. In fact, if you are not careful, once they have grown horns, they can be downright dangerous. It became risky to go into the corral with Batman and he had to be distracted when we wanted to clean up. The most worrying event was when Teresa was in the corral and Batman swished his head and his large horn scraped up Teresa's cheek only an inch from her eye, leaving her with a red welt up her cheek. A very close all.

Batman and Robin were in a corral that is visible from the street, so they became quite an attraction which worried us a little from a safety perspective. What if someone got too close and assumed large cows were just something to hug?

Eventually, much to our surprise, we found a home for Batman and Robin with someone who had always wanted pet cows. It was a good match. We have not had cows again; we are not really set up for it but it was interesting while it lasted.

Chapter 49

THE RACETRACK HORSES

Horses....neigh neigh never

For many years Teresa and I were unable to vacation together. Finding someone to step in and care for 40 to 50 animals every day has always been a challenge. We have had a couple of people up to the task over the years but there have been many periods without such a "Saint", as Bernard wasn't available! Teresa is from Ohio so she could make visits to Ohio while I looked after the animals, and I would go to England while she looked after the animals. I am not suggesting that is an ideal family arrangement, but it was necessary.

One Christmas, about ten years ago as I write, I had gone to England to spend Christmas with my mother, now sadly departed. Teresa had stayed at Modjeska to look after the animals and our daughter Nikki, who was about 15 at the time.

Christmas in Ilkley, in Yorkshire in England, is cool but very pretty. Good food, English beer and bread, and family, made it always an enjoyable trip, despite Mom's failing health due to Parkinson's disease. Even Mom's Parkinson's had a silver lining as it turned out her Parkinson's Doctor was Paul, an old school friend of mine, who I had not seen for about 35 years. We have since renewed our friendship, and in addition he has season tickets to the local football team, Bradford City, so we go to the game when I am back, often with his family, and enjoy beer and curry afterwards. On one occasion when Teresa was with me, she came with us, rather skeptically, to her first ever professional football match. I refuse to call it soccer. She had a lot of fun; she even likes Paul and his family, and Teresa doesn't like many things that don't have fur and 4 legs.

One day while in Ilkley, I received a phone call from Teresa. This was before cheap international cell phone/texting plans, in fact I may have still had a Blackberry as the iPhone had just been launched. Please remember that Blackberry was state of the art not long before! My point is that we did not call/text each other internationally every day as that would have been very expensive.

Teresa started off by telling me that she had been talking to another Rescue which was having trouble and running out of money. I probably made some smart remark like "Tell me something I don't know!" or "And you are telling me this because?" or "How much of our own meagre bank account have you sent them?"

It turned out that Teresa had told this other Rescue that we would help them out by taking 10 of their animals to Modjeska Ranch, which would reduce their operating costs, and of course vastly increase ours.

I asked Teresa what they were, expecting to be told that we had a bunch of dachshunds, or Labradors coming in.

"Thoroughbred Racehorses" she replied! "And one of them is pregnant".

That took me a moment to digest.

We already had a couple of horses, a large quarter horse and a Shetland Pony, and we did have a large pasture and covered corral, but another 10 would be interesting.

When the horses arrived, they were a real mixture. Some had been on the track as recently as a few months before, and been injured, and some were approaching 20 years old. The one thing they had in common was they ranged from quite pretty to stunningly beautiful, and they all had very imaginative names like Phoned Rumor, Katerina's Spirit etc One of them was even descended from Seattle Slew, the Triple Crown winner, and we had all the lineage documents.

Where did they come from? As I said a few came recently from the track, but many came from PMU farms. For those of you with a weak stomach you may want to skip this part of the story. PMU stands for "Pregnant Mare Urine". Until recently in the US, and still in many parts of the world, mares are kept repeatedly pregnant, and their urine is farmed and sold to the pharmaceutical industry to make hormone replacement drugs for menopausal women. I can just imagine that discussion with a doctor, "I am prescribing you racehorse pee to make you feel better".

When the horses arrived, they fitted in quite quickly. We had them checked out by our Horse Veterinarian and they were mostly in decent shape with a few minor ailments here and there apart from one which had a bad case of Laminitis, which is quite serious.

The plan was to find homes for them, and although it took about 3 years, we did so. That included the pregnant mare, which gave birth to a fabulous colt with light beige coloring and white socks and blaze. We named the colt Brooklyn. You may think this is a New York reference, but it is named after

David Beckham's son as David Beckham was playing for the LA Galaxy at the time and Nikki and Teresa were big fans, mostly of how he looks without his shirt on! The mare and colt were adopted out to the same lady who stabled them in a very upmarket community not far from Modjeska. Another was adopted to a retired police officer who eventually moved to North Carolina and took "Kate" with her. As you can imagine, our bill for hay and feed went down a lot once they all had homes!

Here are some pictures of the horses.

"Phoned Rumor"

Brooklyn newborn

Cool Summer

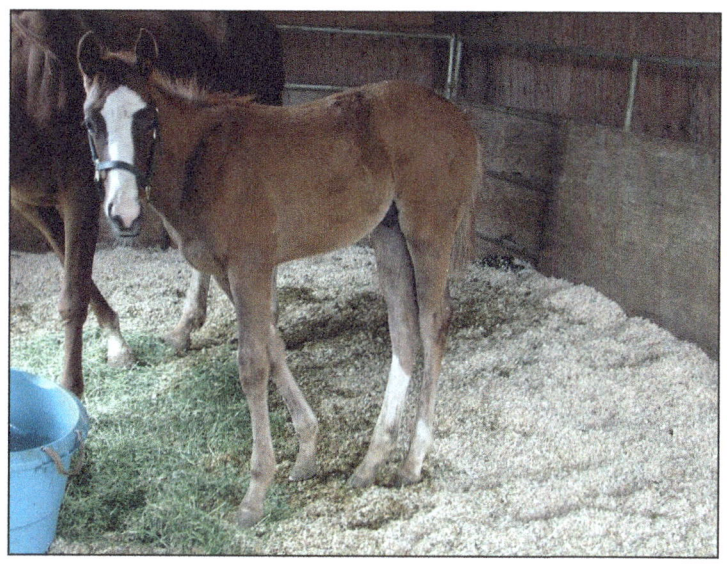

Brooklyn at 3 months old

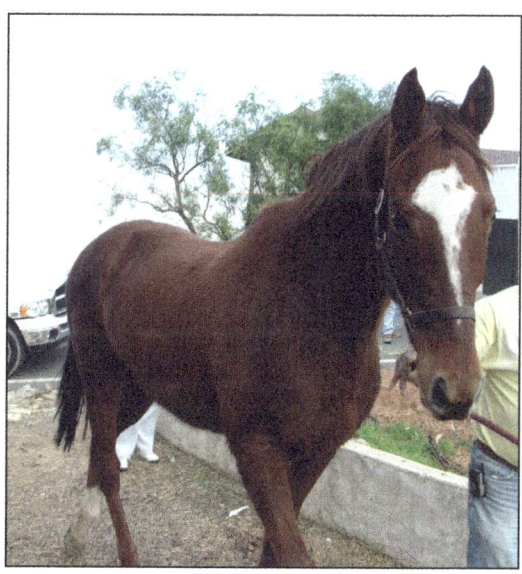

Katerina's Spirit, later "Kate" who went to North Carolina to live.

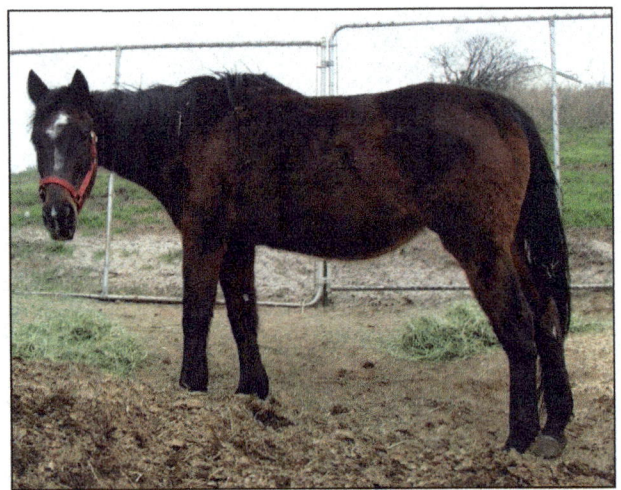

Surely Brilliant

Be True Hold On

Chapter 50

JOVIE HOMELESS BUT LOVED!

One Saturday night, we were called and asked to go to Kaiser Hospital in Anaheim to help a patient's pet, a German Shepherd called Jovie. You may wonder who called us, but I have no recollection, we just seem to be on speed-dial for many people who think we can help when others cannot or will not.

Teresa went to the Hospital, about 25 miles away, and met Jovie's Dad who was in for blood clots in the lungs. Dad, let's call him David, but that's not his name, has MS and now had this extra medical issue, lived in his car, and had no family and no money. I know sometimes we all say, "I don't have any money", but Jovie's Dad literally didn't have any money.

Jovie, a lovable German Shepherd, was with David in the hospital room, but this wasn't allowed by the hospital rules, and they insisted Jovie had to go somewhere else as he is a companion pet but not a documented "service pet", which may have been O.K.

David was very sad to see his buddy leave as Jovie is his only companion. We found out later that David has a daughter on the East Coast and an ex-wife near LA where his 6-year-old daughter lives but his ex-wife will not allow the daughter to see him. That sounds like a very sad life for David.

Teresa assured David that Jovie would be well cared for in Modjeska and that we would reunite them when he was released from hospital which we assumed would be a while as the story was that David would need surgery.

A couple of days later we got a call that David was being released. The problem of course was "released to where?". He was homeless, living in his car and that would not be good for someone recovering from surgery. Teresa decided we could not just let this situation deteriorate as it was bound to do if ignored. As Teresa is "wired" to do she decided we had to find David a place to go, with Jovie, while he recovered. We could not solve his whole homelessness issue, but we could ease the path to health. There were shelters that would take him but none that would let him keep his dog, and Jovie was his life. Teresa worked the phones to find a hotel that would take him and Jovie and give us a good deal if we committed to a month.

We got him into a motel room for a month with Jovie. Teresa went there every week to pay the weekly invoice in advance in cash. It was not the Ritz but it was clean and he had a bathroom and Jovie loved it. We gave David some gift cards for places to eat. Teresa gave him a pet supply store gift card for Jovie's food, and $50.00 cash on the Tuesday as he was released from hospital.

We ran a "Go Fund Me" internet campaign to raise $2,500 to help him get somewhere to stay longer so Jovie and David would not be sleeping in their car. David had applied for disability, but it had been a bureaucratic mess and he was not getting it yet.

As you can see from the picture Jovie loved the bed in the motel. Teresa always says, it takes a village to do this, and we thanked all the donors. Teresa contacted homeless advocates and organizations to make sure David could get back on his feet, despite his medical problems.

Two months went by quickly and we were still paying for the motel.

David said he had got help and would move out of the hotel. This sounded like progress. He was not a great communicator so sometimes we didn't follow the full story.

We found that David and Jovie were back living in his car in a parking lot. Teresa found where he was and took dog food and money for food but it was frustrating that no real progress had been made.

Then David decided to move out of state, where apparently he had a brother of which we were unaware. It is hard when you have medical conditions and would need new Doctors and new appointments. It was tough, but David did it. He packed up, thanked us and headed north.

We were thrilled for both of them. We did hear from him a couple of times and the news was good. We have "rescued" a few people in difficult circumstances along the way while running the Rescue but people do tend to get more complicated than animals.

Jovie in the hotel

Chapter 51

WILD MUSTANGS

Sometimes we get involved in things we didn't anticipate, and which give us pause about our sanity. Wild Mustangs are one of them.

In Northern California there are still herds of wild horses, in Devil's Garden, which is 500 sq miles of rolling hills in the Modoc National Forest. Several years ago it was decided that there were too many mustangs, which was causing overuse of the water and forage for other animals, and a process of rounding up, using helicopters, and selling these mustangs took place. This was very controversial, has been challenged in court, and I am not going to get into the politics of it as it is a whole story in itself that you can look up on Google. I'd like to tell you about our small involvement, which arose from Teresa casually offering, in a phone conversation, to help if she was needed. This was not for the first time I have to say as she has a habit of diving in to help solve animal problems of many kinds, sometimes with forethought of what is involved, and shall we say, sometimes not!

Teresa and I were sat in the kitchen having a bite to eat and a relaxed conversation when she just mentioned "By the way, we have a couple of horses arriving this weekend". "Oh really, what's the story?" I said. Apparently, Teresa had some time earlier been talking to someone involved in rescuing the pregnant mustangs targeted by the roundup in Devil's Garden and had said something like "Well, if you are stuck I can probably take a couple". She had thought nothing more of it, until a long time later when the call came to cash in on her offer.

I asked if we knew just when they were arriving so we could be prepared, although as our knowledge of Mustangs was limited to those made by Ford, preparation would have been very rudimentary. To say that the story was at this point very vague would be accurate. We had been told the trailer would be setting off on Saturday morning, and Teresa assumed that meant they would be arriving on Saturday. However, neither of us knew where Devil's Garden was so we looked it up on Google. It is 720 miles! For perspective that's further than London to Berlin or almost as far as New York to Chicago. California is a big state, and it was obvious that a truck hauling a large horse trailer leaving Devil's Garden sometime Saturday morning was not going to arrive in Modjeska Canyon in Southern California on the same day unless Captain Kirk was driving.

We prepared our front corral which ends only about 10 feet from the street, so unloading would be convenient when the trailer arrived as we were not too sure what to expect.

Late on Sunday we got a call that he was nearly here. We live on a steep narrow hill, the road to which has some tough turns including a tight "hairpin" and in parts a steep 200-foot drop into the canyon on one side. The truck arrived with a very long trailer, which we estimate was 32 feet long, as the driver had pickups to make after dropping off our mustangs. How he maneuvered that beast of a trailer up our street I don't know but I suspect it "wasn't his first rodeo".

The driver pulled to a stop in the street, near the corral but at a 90-degree angle to it as he has just pulled to the side of the road in the dirt, there are no sidewalks. He got out and said to us "How are you going to get these horses from the trailer to the corral?"

We looked at him, then at each other and almost simultaneously said "Oh ****! We thought you would know how to do that. Can we get harnesses on them?"

He was a very grizzly cowboy, a stereotype from central casting off any cowboy TV series, with a Sam Elliott look in his eye. He looked at us as if we were stupid, and he just might have been right.

He said "They are wild horses, only days off the plain, you can't even touch them never mind get a harness on them"

We did wonder what we had volunteered for at this point and probably had thoughts of whether we could turn them and him away, but the look in his eye seemed to suggest that was not an option. This guy has been on the road hauling these horses here for 2 days and they were staying here.

We came up with the idea of removing the whole end piece of the corral which is 12 feet of pipe-rail, and then back the trailer into the corral, so the rear tailgate could be opened for the horses to run out. The challenge was that the truck and trailer were together about 45 feet long and the road is about 12 feet wide.

"Sam Elliott" said he would have to turn the trailer around so it was facing the other way on the street and then he would try to back in. We stood either way on the street to stop traffic, which was mercifully absent, and he managed to back that huge trailer 90 degrees into a narrow driveway and into the corral. Demonstrations of immense skill in any undertaking are always amazing to watch and this was no exception. If you think you know how to tow and reverse a trailer, I strongly doubt you could have done this, in one smooth move, it was truly impressive and left a feeling of awe and respect, or a mental thought of "Holy **** I could NEVER do that"

"Sam Elliott" released the horses which ran to the other end of the corral, where we had put down hay, and then he pulled out while we replaced the end piece of the corral. At this point "Sam" was in a much better mood and we chatted for a few minutes before he said he had more pickups to do so he had better get on the road.

The Mustangs were beautiful, both pregnant, one a mid-chestnut and one a darker chestnut, both with jet black manes. We named them Thelma and Louise, after two other wild women, although they drove a Thunderbird in the movie, not a Mustang unfortunately. If we approached the horses they would run as far away as they could. It took months until we could touch one of them and then only very gently.

Our neighbor, Rusty Richards, who is in the cowboy Hall of Fame, sang with the Sons of the Pioneers, and was a stuntman on "How they Won the West" and many other things, came up and spent a long time telling us what it takes to train a wild mustang. He has done it many times. One of the first things you need is a ROUND horse pen. We do not have that, and while we have a lot of land, in Orange County terms anyway, it is not flat and not suited to this task.

Our short-term priority was to let the mares give birth and then find them all a home. As Rusty had told us we would need a circular corral and a lot of time and patience, that's just three things Teresa and I are short of to go alongside lack of experience.

One April morning, the first foal was born to Thelma. Just a stunning black filly who frolicked in the corral. We called her Brooklyn. It was tempting just to spend the day watching her. "Mom" was protective, and we could not touch, but 3 months later, we could stroke and brush Brooklyn while "Mom" watched cautiously. Brooklyn was an attention seeker.

Six weeks after Brooklyn, Louise gave birth to a beautiful filly we named Spirit. Unfortunately Spirit never warmed up like Brooklyn and was skittish all the time we had her.

Moms are protective of children, and mares are protective of their foals too. One day, we had a visitor to the Rescue, and they were fascinated by the mustangs, having been horse people all their lives. Teresa, however, was careful to make sure they did not get too close, as although these mustangs looked beautiful, they were still not domesticated, if not totally wild. While trying to keep the visitor from getting too close Teresa herself got a little close herself and turned her back. Louise bit her on the head, tore out a large clump of hair, broke the skin and gave Teresa a hell of a headache. It could have been worse of course but it was a painful reminder that one must be careful around animals and especially when they have their offspring nearby.

As you may have read earlier in this book, we did rescue a lot of horses ten years before, but they were all trained racehorses totally comfortable around people. The mustangs were a different challenge.

As time wore on and the fillies grew, we knew we did not have the facilities for 4 grown mustangs. Teresa researches animal issues all the time, and eventually said she had been in touch with an operation which specializes in the rescue and training of mustangs and nothing else. They have 35 acres and were about a 3-hour drive away. Like all rescues, they were short of money, but they were enthusiastic about taking all four of our mustangs. We gave them a $1500 donation out of our own very limited Rescue funds and paid $500 for the transport. If that surprises you then put it in the context of how much it cost us to keep and feed them. The old adage someone "eats like a horse" is illustrated every day with mustangs who eat more than normal horses. On advice we fed the mustangs "Orchard" hay and between them they ate two bales a day. $34/ bale! We had them for about a year. A year at $68/day is around $25,000.

Knowing the saga of getting the mustangs into the corral when they arrived, the prospect of getting them out again was a daunting one, and just who could we get to transport them? A "horsey" neighbor suggested someone they knew, and we arranged to have the horses picked up at 4.30am one morning. Why the early hour? We would have to block traffic while we loaded. Teresa was concerned also about lighting as it would still be dark and worried that turning on bright lights would spook the horses, so we set up floodlights and left them on all night.

At 4.30, "Joe" turned up with his long horse trailer, and the neighbors came over to help. Only one of the horses was people friendly, and that was the older filly, Brooklyn. The other three gave us nightmares if we ended up with wild horses escaping and running around the canyon. Joe backed up to the corral from the blocked street and we again removed the 12-foot end piece of the corral, while the horses gathered at the far end wondering what was going on. Joe opened the back doors and put down the ramp. He threw some hay in the far front end of the trailer. The three horses we were worried about just ran into the trailer and started eating. Wow, we thought, it can't be that easy.

However, our lovely friendly Brooklyn was still stood at the far end of the corral not moving. No encouragement seemed to work, we tried treats, we tried stroking her and saying silly things that of course she could not understand. Joe managed to wrestle a harness onto her head and pulled her, but no dice. At some points Joe and Brooklyn looked like a wrestling match from TV. We were not sure whether to find it funny or not as we didn't want Joe to get hurt. Joe must have been 250 lbs of muscle but Brooklyn was having none of it. This went on for about 20 minutes with Joe literally trying to put his arms around the horse and make some progress.

Finally, Joe managed to get a rope behind Brooklyn's legs to augment the harness and with a lot of struggle and pushing Brooklyn very reluctantly inched into the trailer where I quickly closed the door with Joe inside.

After getting Joe out of the trailer, it was "job done". It was now light, and we needed to open the street! Off went the truck and trailer and we all breathed a huge sigh of relief. Thanks Joe.

Beautiful beasts, just stunning. Glad we were able to rescue them and get them to a good place. If you have not already done so, Google the story behind the horses of Devils Garden in California.

Thelma and Louise

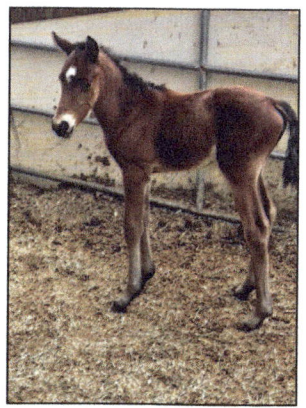 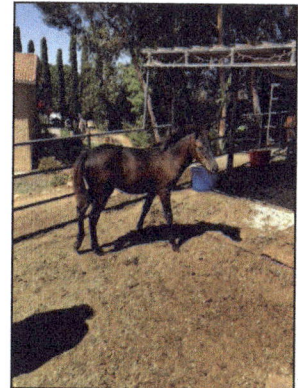

Brooklyn   Spirit

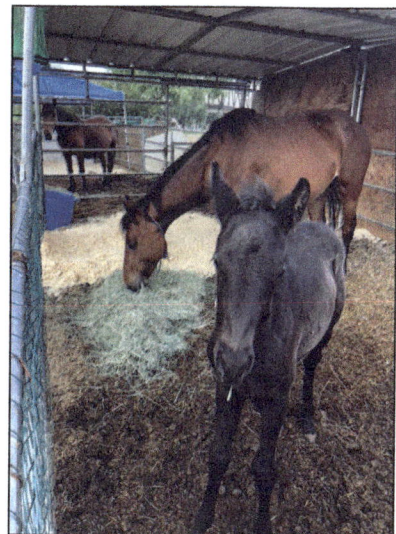 

Spirit and her Mom Louise at Modjeska Ranch Rescue and then at their new home 2 years later

Spirit grown up at at new home

Chapter 52

THE RESCUE GETS SHEEPISH

We get a lot of calls, emails and texts from people who want us to take animals. We must be selective not only from the perspective of our physical capacity but also our financial and mental capacity. You would not believe how often people get irritated with us if we can't help them, "Well you're a rescue so you HAVE to take him, and we are leaving on vacation, so it has to be today! And no, we can't afford to give you a donation, we pay our taxes and I'm sure you get support from public sources somewhere!" (We don't!).

We've even had an offer to "donate" a nice purebred dog, and then they say, "We spent $1,000 to buy the dog so will you give us $1,000 since that's what it's worth." I will not assault your ears with our visceral reaction to such a statement, but the simplified answer is "No".

One day we got a call from someone we know well and like who has also been involved in Rescue and has generously helped us often, so we felt an obligation to help if we could.

In essence they had been alerted to a neighbor of theirs who had sheep which had been acquired to keep the grass down in a large yard. The sheep were not doing their job, the neighbors were not feeding them, having assumed they would eat the grass, and in fact were using them for paintball practice. Could we take 2 sheep if they could persuade the owners to release them? Well, as it happens, over the years we have had many kinds of animal but not sheep and Teresa always quite fancied having sheep. So we said yes, well Teresa said yes, and I was informed of the decision.

On the designated day, transport was arranged to bring the sheep about 40 miles to the Rescue. When they arrived in a truck, we didn't get two sheep. We got one large curly-horned Ram and 3 pregnant Ewes!

Not long after arrival the Ewes started to give birth. One of them gave birth to twins. So now we have a ram, 3 ewes and 4 lambs. One morning I went up to feed and saw one of the lambs curled up motionless in a corner, apparently dead. Teresa distracted the sheep while I went in to get the dead lamb. Distraction was necessary as the ram was really large with horns that curled in a full circle, and he liked to ram the fence He had got out once and rammed me in the thigh having run at me from about 6 feet. Very painful.

I picked up the lamb. He was not dead. Apparently, it is not unusual for a ewe to feed one lamb and reject the other. This was what had happened. What do we do with a 2-day old lamb, what do they eat, where do we keep it? All good questions to which we had no answers, but Google is very useful. The lamb, now named Bruce, was about 9 inches high and very cute. We did hear lots of lamb chop jokes from friends or maybe were they not jokes?

Bruce came to live in the kitchen with the small dogs. He was bottle-fed with goat's milk, 2 cartons a day at $5 a carton, so $70 a week just to feed Bruce! He grew quickly and of course thought he was a dog. He became very friendly and loved to be held. If we sat on the couch to watch TV Bruce and 2 or 3 dogs would be there with us. He also liked to eat the paint off the walls. I had painted the walls with semi-gloss paint but probably had not prepared properly by pre-sanding, so it could be peeled, and our kitchen wall started to look dappled. I of course assured the Environmental Protection Agency that there was no lead paint involved so no animal cruelty could be alleged!

It was easy to forget that Bruce was a ram. His Dad was a large, curly-horned, bad-tempered ram, but Bruce was so cute, well for at least a while he was cute.

We had found a home for the other sheep at a farm which invited families with PTSD victims to mix with animals in a rural setting, but Bruce was still with us. These sheep were Dorper sheep which are meat sheep and are self-shedding, so they do not have to sheared. Bruce eventually grew too big to be in the house, and to be honest, too smelly! His transition to being in the corral with goats and horses was not too bad although one got the feeling that each time we saw him he was expecting to go "back home". His wool does self-shear but not completely, so he developed a sort of mullet hairdo because the wool on the top did not come off, only that on the sides. I am sure he thinks he looks great.

In conclusion, a lamb is a fun house pet and off the charts in the cuteness scale; however, a fully-grown ram is NOT a house pet. I know quite a few people who think goats are good in the house, but a ram is not something I favor. Bruce lived happily with the goats in the back corral for three years and had many fans who would always want pictures in email and Facebook updates on his health. If you want to know what happened then, read the chapter on the 2020 fires.

Bruce as a cute house lamb

Bruce's Father!!!!

Bella and Buffy

It was a very sad night here at Modjeska Ranch when we lost Bella the black and white Great Dane. Bella came to us with huge tumors hanging almost all the way down to the ground underneath her. I know that sounds almost unbelievable, but it is true. She had been over-bred and had lots of cancerous tumors. We had 2 surgeries done on her to remove as much as possible and she was a joy to have around the place, getting on well with all the other dogs and being a real attention hound. After a while the cancer returned very aggressively with new tumors appearing inside and on the surface and leaking. That's why in some pictures you see her wearing a T-Shirt. The time came when we could see she was in pain, and it was time to take the pain away.

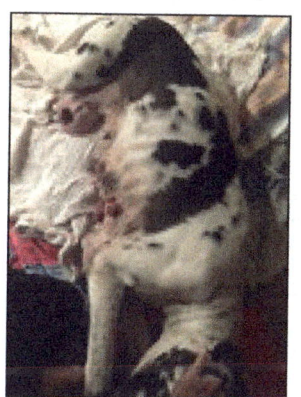 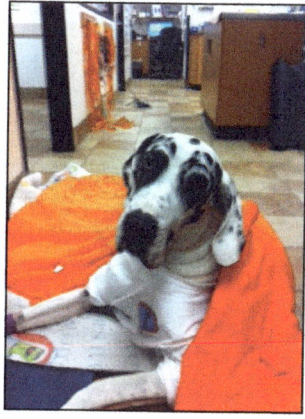

Bella in a shirt after second surgery

By Russell Taylor

Some while after losing Bella we took in Buffy, who had similar issues, as you can see. We had surgery done on Buffy and she lived at the Rescue happily for a few years until nature took its course.

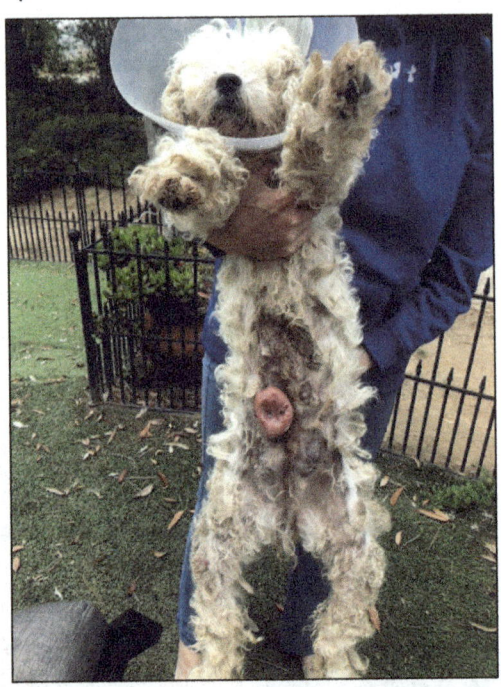

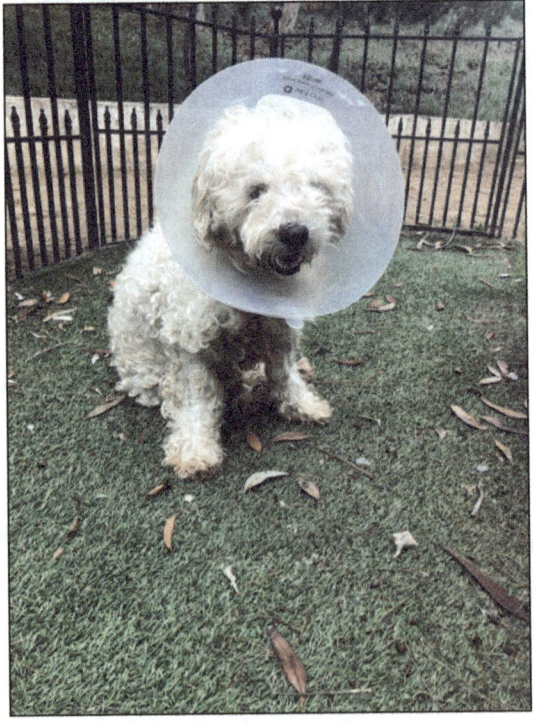

Chapter 53

FRUSTRATION...RETURNEES AND ATTITUDES

One of the sad and frustrating experiences of Rescue is when an animal has been adopted out and comes back. We do our best to select only good homes and if in doubt, we make an excuse and keep them at Modjeska. However, it is understandable if a new animal doesn't fit or cannot settle with their other pets and when that happens in the first couple of weeks, we understand.

This is Chooie. He is a ten-year-old Lab mix we took into the Rescue in January 2012. He was going blind and needed a safe loving home. He fitted in at the Ranch and seemed happy. A family came to see Chooie; they had heard the story and wanted to adopt him. They had experience with blind dogs. Normally Teresa will not adopt out animals with medical issues as the expense can be too much for a family, and a blind dog can get confused by too many changing environments. However, in this case, we gave in and let the family take Chooie because they were very convincing in their determination to give Chooie a great home for his golden years despite his blindness.

You know how this story ends already, don't you?

Chooie was brought back to us after about 15 months in his other home. Not a week or two but 15 months! So now we had to get him used to another new environment yet again. He was very sweet and friendly and settled down after some adjustment time, but the return after 15 months left us very frustrated.

In about 2006 we adopted out a lovely Bassett Hound. He was brought back after 6 YEARS! "It's not working out" was the excuse. Really! After 6 years! Running a rescue can challenge one's faith in human nature.

Many people express their understanding and admiration for what we do. Some express a burning desire to do the same thing "if only they had money and land". I resist my urge to smile when people say this.

Chapter 54

THE 2007 FIRE

October 21st, 2007, was our daughter Nikki's 14th birthday. It was a Sunday. At her request we went to a Japanese restaurant for dinner as we all like the Teppan style food and the great show from the chef that always comes with it. Nikki at the time was vegetarian but Teppan veggies are very good.

Towards the end of dinner, some people at a neighboring table recognized us as the "Modjeska Ranch Rescue People" , which happens quite a lot, and came over in some state of concern. "There is a fire in Modjeska Canyon, you should go home now".

We assured them that small fires in the canyons were not uncommon, and we were sure that there was no need for concern. They were not convinced but didn't press the matter.

A little while later we left and drove home, or almost home. The police had closed the roads to the canyon! We were in a line of cars, including our neighbors, trying to get through and also trying to find out what was happening. The police had orders not to admit anyone at all. The main canyon road from Modjeska to Silverado, about 6 miles, was closed.

About an hour later, residents of Modjeska were allowed access by showing ID. We got home and could see lots of smoke but could not see the fire itself yet. It was clear that the situation was dangerous. There was not yet a mandatory evacuation, but our particular circumstances with all the animals would not enable us to evacuate very quickly should the time come. We had on the wall a list of people with horse trailers who had offered to help should this situation ever arise, and we decided that night that the animals needed to go first thing in the morning. At first light we loaded up horses and goats in trailers. Where does one take them, you may ask? Well, we had friends who ran a stable in Coto De Caza, Maxwell's Stables, run by John and Jilly, who were life savers. All the horses and goats went there and were well looked after for about a month. Thank you, thank you John and Jilly.

The fire was getting closer, had jumped the main canyon road, and was visible about half a mile from the house. At this point it was covering thousands of acres and probably 5 miles long. Seeing flames that are 30 feet high a short distance from your house is a sobering experience. This confirmed to us that we should evacuate, even though it was so far "recommended" but not mandatory. We had many friends and supporters who had offered to take in dogs and cats to help us so we shuttled them around to safe areas. The remaining ten dogs were split into two groups as I went to stay with friends and took 5 dogs with me and Teresa went to stay with other friends and took 5 dogs with her. Beware becoming our friends.

When we got to our friend's houses, I suddenly thought "I didn't get our passports. They are in my office". I told Teresa I would go back for them. She was livid that I would even consider going back, it was far too dangerous. However, of course I decided to go. I would just pull into the driveway, dash into the office and then get back out of there. I drove to the house in my little black Infiniti G35 sports car. I pulled into the driveway and dashed into the office. I found the papers and ran back to the car.

I stopped dead still in the driveway. I had a flat tire! I must have driven over a nail or something else sharp. I could see the fire and it was getting far too close. I would have to change the wheel. I got out the spare wheel and the jack and the wheel brace. Oh dear, fancy wheels like mine have lug locks so they cannot be stolen. In the car should be the special attachment to enable me to take off the wheel. Had I ever used it? Did I even know where it was? Of course not! Two minutes of panic rifling through the car to find the lug lock fitting ended up with no luck. What to do? I called my friend Guy at whose house I was bunking with the dogs. Guy is very practical and is from New Jersey. Guys called Guy from New Jersey KNOW how to do stuff. He said, "I'll be there in five". He was there in five. Guy knelt by the flat tire with a large hammer and some metal contraption. He said, "Look away, you don't want to see what I'm doing to your expensive wheel". Literally, a bang, another bang, and the wheel lug-nut was off. We changed the wheel and screamed out of there "burning rubber". Make sure you know someone called Guy or someone from New Jersey, they can be life savers.

The next day was Tuesday. We stood on a hill looking towards the canyons and the only thing visible was smoke, some white, some black, billowing into the sky. If we looked a little to the right, we could see flames spreading along the back on the hills above a newer housing development. These very expensive houses were on little cul-de-sacs spreading up the hills, and the flames were right up against their rear fences. It was hard to measure but the flames looked huge, maybe 50 feet high.

We spent some time that day in the friend's house where Teresa was staying. The TV had wall to wall coverage of the fire. At one point the County Fire Captain came on the screen. He said, "We have pulled all of our people out of Modjeska Canyon, it's just too dangerous". Teresa had been stoic up to this point but lost it and cried when it looked like the canyon was going to be destroyed. I had never seen her affected that way before as she normally handles difficult situations with strength and defiance.

It turned out later that some of the volunteer fire fighters from the Modjeska Volunteer fire station went back in to fight for the canyon. More to follow on that.

The fire raged on for days. The canyons looked to be lost and TV channels were showing pictures, but information was still sketchy, there was so much smoke that nothing could be seen. Our dogs of course just thought they were on vacation and why were we all stressed out and in tears, and where was their food.

By Friday we had been gone from the house for 4 days and the fire was not under control according to the news. We had accepted by this time that the house was gone.

My phone rang. "Hi this is Jamie, Alex's son, I am at your house. I just put out some fire on the hay, but the house is still here". I asked him what else was still there on the street and in the canyon, but he said the smoke was too thick to see very far. Jamie worked for animal control who had people evacuating stray animals and he was also the son of the neighbor directly across the street. Their house was still there. However, he said the house just 50 yards up the street, our friend's geodesic dome house, was gone completely, right down to the concrete slab; it was just smoldering ash.

We had feared the worst with our neighbor's house as the TV stations had repeatedly shown their llamas running around the hills. Makes for good TV. After this was all over the Llamas lived at our place with the horses for 2 ½ years while our neighbors rebuilt their house.

The fires hit the canyon hard, sparing our home but tragically taking those of 4 neighbors on our street. 10 houses in total were destroyed in our canyon, but that was a miracle. I still do not really know how the houses and the hundreds of overhanging trees that line the canyon survived, apart from knowing that the firefighters did an amazing job, risking life and limb to save the historic canyon. Helena Modjeska's house, built in 1888 and designed by Stanford White and surrounded by trees, was untouched. (Look up architect Stanford White and his life for a very lively story)

We were evacuated for 8 days! The house was structurally ok but completely covered inside and out with smoke-soot and debris. We had to live in an RV for a month in the driveway while we cleaned up the house.

Then came the rains and evacuation orders due to mudslide dangers. No plagues of frogs though. For those of you who do not live in fire danger areas, the problem after the fire is that all the ground cover is gone. When the rains come, there is nothing to slow it down and allow it to soak into the land. In a canyon type environment, this can produce flash floods and debris flows. You may think that is not bad, but a debris flow can literally be many feet high, developing and rushing into the canyon in minutes. They are so dangerous that, after fire evacuation, there can be rain evacuations!

The silver lining to all this is that some of the dogs who were evacuated found permanent homes where they had been "billeted", and the TV news coverage found more. Kona our Great Pyrenees was seen on Channel 5 news and now lives near Malibu in luxury. Emily the Basset who had been here for over a year also got a home! Sadly, Daphne the St Bernard with Addison's disease, died shortly after returning from evacuation, probably a stress-related end. She got home, having spent a month evacuated with a friend of ours. She walked into our house, lay down and died. That was very upsetting.

On returning home we found a number of our patio chairs lined up in the back yard. It turned out that some of the Firefighters had stationed themselves in our back yard. That was maybe because we are high up and have a good view of the surrounding areas. I should have told them where the beer was! They deserve it.

Chapter 55
WRITTEN AFTER A LOT OF RAIN

*A weekend at Modjeska Ranch with rain, floods, stray dogs on the counter,
escaped goats, garage cleaning, skittish horses and ....and gravel and finches.*

It's been an eventful few days in the canyons, and not just for the Rescue. The usually dry creeks look like fast running rivers and are beautiful in their way, but also problematic as most of us are simply not prepared for such a deluge. We are lucky that the Rescue is high up on a hill.

The storms do give me back-ache though You may well ask why that should be the case? Well, the street on which the Rescue stands is steep, and each year the County unloads loose sand and gravel into the trench by the side of the road outside our house. This is apparently to keep the rain directed down the street and into run-offs designed to funnel the water down into a creek rather than creating problems of ground movement and erosion. However, each year the rain simply washes a lot of this gravel and sand out of the trench and into our driveway, ending up with a 9-to-12-inch gravel bank at the entrance gate, over which we have to drive to get in, and leaving once again deep gravel trenches by the side of the street. I shovel all of this very heavy and wet sand and gravel mix out of the driveway so we can get in and out, and I have to do it when it is wet. If I don't get to it until later in the year, then the sun turns it almost to concrete and I need a pickaxe to move it. It will save on a gym membership if anyone wants some weight training. When the weather is as "inclement" as it has been, the dogs want to stay inside. All 27 or so of them! We encourage them to still go out for their "needs" but as you can imagine, if we are not looking, some of them get lazy. Just as well we have tile floors, bleach in buckets and lots of towels. I've told you about towels before. We use them to dry things but also use the old ones to clean the floors by pouring hot dilute bleach and water on the tile then standing on a towel and resurrecting the old dance "The Twist", some of you will know what I mean and the rest of you are too young. The challenge is magnified when we have new dogs that are not acclimated yet to the Modjeska "pack". Last week, some of you will know we "rescued" a couple of dogs running in the canyon. One of them is a young Shepherd, perhaps mixed with a little husky. Very pretty dog, but a little skittish still. We have him mainly in the kitchen with his buddy and a couple of the small dogs. Well, we have found out that, if we are not in the kitchen, then nothing on the counters is safe! Bags, pills, food, paper, clothing will end up on the floor. It is not destroyed, just "redistributed". Also last week you may remember we took in 2 pregnant wild mustangs. The rumors that we are crazy are obviously true! It's a long story. We have the horses in our front corral which has a cover and a large wooden dividing wall across the middle (with room for them to get by). Being recently wild horses, they do not seem to mind the weather at all but they are still not used to humans. One of them is settling in well and seems more relaxed but the other one is taking more time. Well, for some reason something must have spooked them, as they have knocked down the wall. It is not a major problem; it just means they do not have as much enclosed shelter as we wanted but they are doing OK. We cannot go into the stall yet so it will just have to stay there lying on the ground for the moment, it is not dangerous. An interesting point is that we are feeding them "Orchard" hay which they like, but if we throw in carrots, they don't really care, whereas normally carrots are like chocolate to a horse.

While this is happening on this rainy Sunday, I am feeding the horses and goats and the sheep, and I suddenly realized we are a goat short. Then I see, on the very far side of the pasture, there is a goat on the OTHER side of the fence enjoying the sweet wet grass. And it's just starting to rain again. I call Teresa out, as getting a goat back in is not a one-man job. I manage to walk all the way round and down the hill, so I am behind the goat, and I shoo him up the hill towards Teresa who has a leash ready. This works well. However, getting the goat into the back corral will entail going past the wild horses, which is not a good idea. There is a small passage we could use but it is at present filled with 10 plastic wrapped bales of wood shavings, ready for when it stops raining so we can fix the muddy corals. Now we need to move the shaving bales, which are only reasonably heavy but moving them fast is awkward. Anyway, the job gets done, goat back in the corral, and after the rain I will have to go "riding fences" again to find out where he got out. I can sing "Desperado" while I am doing it.

Yesterday, Saturday, Teresa was working her job at the Vet office and our garage, a storage area of course, had become a mess as we are both too busy to keep it organized, so as there was a break in the rain, I tore the place apart and bleached it and threw a lot of things away. Always a fun job.

In our kitchen are new arrivals, 2 tiny finches which Teresa brought home a few weeks ago. As is the circle of life, there are now also 3 tiny baby birds in the hanging nest. They are very active and like to throw birdseed all over the place, but they are a change of pace from all of our large animals. The birds seem to breed often, constantly laying eggs, so I think we may have to make egg removal a routine. I wonder what they taste like. I can tell you that's a joke as, even when we had rescued chickens that laid perfectly good eggs, Teresa would not allow them to be eaten which is a shame. I am told fresh eggs taste really good!

Chapter 56

THANKSGIVING AT MRR

Thanksgiving 2016 at Modjeska Ranch Rescue started early. It was 2am, dark and cold, when Teresa woke me. I admit that Teresa would be woken by an ant sneezing in the next town, whereas I would not wake up unless you slap a wet towel on my face while turning on AC/DC at full volume. She blurted out something about the pig and urged me to get up quickly and accompany her out into the dark and cold outside. I knew better than to ask for a more detailed explanation. Love, honor and OBEY! I said something like "I'll be right there my darling!" I may have used other words.

On reaching the corral the noise Teresa had heard became apparent. We used to have 8 pigs. Over the last years, the number of pigs has dwindled through the normal aging process, to the point where there was only one left. He lived in a section of the corral set out for him, although he could go into the other areas if he chose. Well, it seemed that, this night, he had got out of his area and into the larger area occupied by a large horse and some goats. The pig was having a hissy fit at one of the horses and squealing up a storm, loud enough that Teresa had heard from the house resulting in our disturbed sleep. Now we do expect a little huffing and puffing and jealousy around feeding time morning and night, but a 2 am fuss is unusual. Teresa had a flashlight, but I turned on the corral lights, which Teresa says she cannot reach despite being taller than me. Food of course is usually the key to getting an animal to do as you wish, and our objective was to get the pig back into his area in his little house, which requires him to get under a pipe corral fence. He manages this himself just fine when it is his idea, but of course when it is our idea, he pretends he can't do it! Teresa had to "herd" him, have you ever tried to herd a pig, while I literally lifted a section of pipe corral fencing which is very heavy. A loaf of bread trailed out over our intended route eventually got Mr. Pig back where he was supposed to be, and he settled down in his igloo to chew on my breakfast toast-bread. All this of course while also keeping the large horse and 4 goats from noisily interfering in the whole process.

We returned to bed around 3am, which is about 2 hours before Teresa gets up to start the morning feeding. I get to "sleep in" until 5.45 or even 6 before starting my chores. The morning feeding normally starts with lots of bowls set out on the kitchen island, which are duly filled with dog food, cat food, grated cheese, chicken breast, rice etc according to the needs of the day and the health of the animals. Some of the dogs mill around while some just continue to doze until it's time to put down the full bowls. Well, on the morning of Thanksgiving, one of the sleeping dogs was very still. It soon became apparent that he was not asleep but had passed away during the night. This is always sad; however, when running a rescue which has three-quarters of its occupants as what you might term "seniors", it is not unusual. It was a very old Bassett. He was a nice old soul, if a little grouchy at times. We have a soft spot for Bassetts having had one ourselves before starting the Rescue.

So that was a sad start to the lovely holiday we call Thanksgiving, but, as I said, it is something we deal with on a regular basis. At least he got some TLC and relaxation in his final months.

Chapter 57

RUNNING AROUND THE CANYON

I have written elsewhere about chasing Spirit the Shetland pony. He was Spirit by name and nature and had no respect for my attempts to catch him on steep grassy and dusty hills while dressed in a white dress shirt, dress pants and leather-soled loafers. I have always been quite athletic for my age (he said modestly!) but changing direction while running in leather-soled shoes on a steep grassy hill is a magic trick I have not yet perfected, so I would fall a lot and my khaki dress pants would end up with grass stains than made them resemble army camouflage. Spirit seemed to think this was fun. I was of another opinion.

You may ask "Why was Spirit out of his pasture/corral in the first place?" Good question. On the rare occasions this happened it would sometimes be that someone, me or a volunteer, had failed to latch/chain the gate properly and had not realized the mistake. When you open/close these gates every day, now and again you get careless and don't double check. Speaking of not closing the gate properly I think we all have those things we do so often that muscle memory takes over and it is not a conscious action, so even if we do it wrong we don't even notice.

216

Another fun Spirit story was when our neighbors the Carters had a birthday party one weekend. Being rodeo/horse people, they invited a "cowboy" poet to attend and recite poetry and tell stories. None of us can remember his name but he had a tall round-topped cowboy hat and some missing fingers having been a cowboy since he was very young. The party went well, and the music, poetry and stories were great. The poet must have stayed overnight. The next day our Shetland pony, Spirit, got out again, not only out of the corral but onto the street. We could not catch him and more and more ex-partygoers tried to help until there were enough people to surround the horse but at some distance. All this was still in the middle of the street. Nobody could get close to the horse which would bolt whenever anyone got close, and all the hollering and verbal encouragement from the crowd didn't seem to help.

Out came the cowboy, dressed like a cowboy from "Rawhide" or "The Rifleman". He shouted, "Everyone shut up and stand absolutely still". Everyone obeyed. He also stood very still. We all stood very still for what seemed like ages but was probably 3 or 4 minutes. The horse also stood still and was still surrounded at a distance of 20 yards by the crowd.

Then the cowboy slowly walked up the horse, slid a halter over the horse's head and led him back to the corral.

As my mother used to say "Everything is difficult, until you know how, and then it's easy!"

If the goats or pigs get out it is more often a failed fence issue and I have to walk the fences to find the problem, which may seem a simple task if you have never done it. If you have done it, then you will know the urge to use very bad language when you find nothing wrong with the fence although you KNOW that there is something wrong, so you walk it again and again and again then you patch where you think they are getting out, and the next day they are out again, at which point you use really, really, bad language. Billy, a small pigmy goat with big horns, can hook his horns under chain-link fence, work it up, squeeze under the fence, and leave it looking as if nothing has been touched. What a talent.

In the early years of the Rescue, which we started in 2001, we seemed to have more "doggie escapees" than in later years. Of course, the layout of fences and gates probably improved as we grew in experience, but sometimes we would have a dog or two who could have escaped from Leavenworth without breaking a sweat. Huskies are very smart. For some reason there were years where we seemed to take a lot of one breed, and one year it was Huskies. We probably had 30 dogs and 5 of them were Huskies. They can climb a six-foot fence, and while they were friendly, they liked being able to take off into the canyon. I remember one incident where they had managed to get onto the other side of the Canyon, about a mile away, onto a large piece of hilly land and it was a 3-hour ordeal to catch them. Another time they went down the hill to a neighbor's house (Rusty Richards, I have mentioned him before). Having located the dog at Rusty's house, it proceeded just to circle the house with me in hot pursuit, again and again and again!

Another story of inappropriate footwear relates to Teresa suddenly shouting, "There are horses running on the back road". For context we have three driveways and one of them is a dirt road leading alongside the house and curving along the back of the house and then down to a neighbor's property. The horses were running along the back road away from the neighbor's house and towards our street which is paved, narrow and steep. The road does not have a lot of traffic but what traffic it does have can sometimes be going too fast down the steep incline which has an almost cliff-like drop off on one side. Even bicycles race down the road at crazy speeds and running into a horse would be unhealthy at best for both parties. Our first concern was whether these were our horses, although we didn't know how that could be. We ran out and saw the horses belonged to our neighbor at the back, who had not yet realized they were gone. We ran to our corral to get halters and ropes and took off after the horses which had turned down the steep street.

I need to add an "aside" here. For a while I worked in Switzerland in a hotel. I took to wearing backless wooden clogs which I found very comfortable and practical. I still buy and wear backless wooden clogs by preference. Of course, on this day I was wearing backless wooden clogs! While I think they are great footwear, they are not good for running or grip, especially on a steep tarmac road.

I ran as best I could down the hill after these horses, hoping they did not get hurt, or hurt someone else, and that I did not break an ankle. Teresa came too. Near the bottom of the hill is a tight blind turn, but you can go straight on into the curving driveway of Rusty and Amy's house, which is on ten acres. The horses headed there which was good. At the bottom of the driveway the horses stopped. Rusty's corrals and trucks were there, and I tried to get ropes and halters on the horse although Teresa told me I was crazy to try this while wearing clogs. As usual she was right. I would get a rope on a horse and then the horse would simply drag me around in the dirt because I had no grip. Everyone watching thought this very funny, although was concerned I may get hurt. Eventually, the horse's owner arrived and he and Rusty, who were riding buddies, managed to control the horses and get them back to where they were supposed to be.

Another day, our neighbor Diane arrived in our driveway in her "Rhino" (like an industrial golf cart) and told me to jump in as her Llamas were missing and we needed to find them. Diane and her husband Jim are good friends and run a company called American Horse Products, which I have mentioned before. This tells you they are knowledgeable animal people, but they can still lose Llamas! We went behind our house down the trail, but no sign, then raced down the street to the bottom of the canyon and drove all the streets, looking for llamas, as one often does of course. No sign of them could we find, so as we were coming back up the steep Grade Rd., a number of neighbors were gathered where they had found the llamas in a front yard eating the plants. The animals were quite content and almost on the front porch. Now, how do you catch a llama who is quite content and doesn't want to be caught? The street was a single file street leading to only another 3 houses, so we roped off the street just past the house in question and at the intersection with the Grade Rd., while we tried to get ropes around the llamas. One would think their long necks would make this easy, but I assure you it is not if they don't want to be caught. We could get within a few feet, and they would move. Rusty Richards lived next door and he prepared to lasso the llamas. Then the neighbor who was farther down the street decided he wanted to drive out, so he drove his car right up to the rope and got very agitated with everyone even though he could see what we were trying to do. We had to stop catching the llamas and move the ropes for him He was not very popular, and a few unladylike words were heard amongst the gathered llama catchers. Eventually Rusty and Diane got ropes around the neck of the "lead" llama and Diane said the others will follow, and they did, allowing us to get ropes around them also. Then we walked all the llamas up the steep road back to Diane's house which was a bizarre sight. Modjeska Canyon looked like Peru for a short while with about 8 people and 4 llamas on ropes in the middle of the road.

Chapter 58

THE STORY OF KODIAK AS TOLD BY TERESA

3 year old German Shepherd Saved by 3 hours!

Kodiak was headed to be euthanized by her owner. She had started to display increased aggression to the family's other dogs and they were worried about their grandchildren. They had already set the appointment for euthanasia at 4am on the 8th September.

I spoke to the owner, and realized after 30 minutes of conversation that Kodiak needed a second chance. Kodiak has an eye condition called Pannus; this disease is found quite often in the Shepherd breed and results eventually in blindness. However, eye medication twice a day can slow its progression.

Once I got off the phone I started to get ready for a new member of the "family" at our home which is Modjeska Ranch Rescue. The owner drove Kodiak down from Acton, California. Kodiak was nervous, but fine with me. That was September 9th 2012.

As you can see Kodiak did really well with her new family and friends and doesn't mind her twice-daily medication at all. We had her eyes checked out and yes, she may lose her sight, but she will adjust. In the meantime she has love, peace and a family at Modjeska.

One of my favorite pictures from early days at the Rescue

"You wash and I'll dry"

Yoko was a beautiful white Akita with a great personality, but a loner as far as most of the other dogs were concerned. Most of the "Arctic" dogs have a hierarchy which is them at the top, humans next and other dogs below that. This day "Dobie" was helping in the kitchen. Yoko was with us for many years. We did get her adopted a couple of times, but it never seemed to work out and she would come back. I guess she liked us.

By Russell Taylor

<u>Another Christmas at Modjeska Ranch Rescue</u>

Everyone being well behaved and hoping Santa brings something tasty

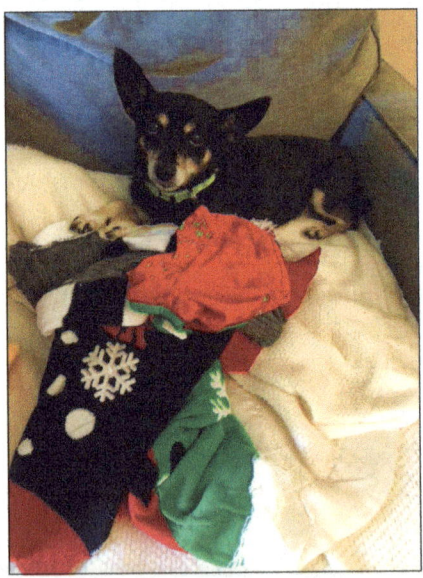

Parker deciding which Christmas outfit to wear

Car Crash Hannah

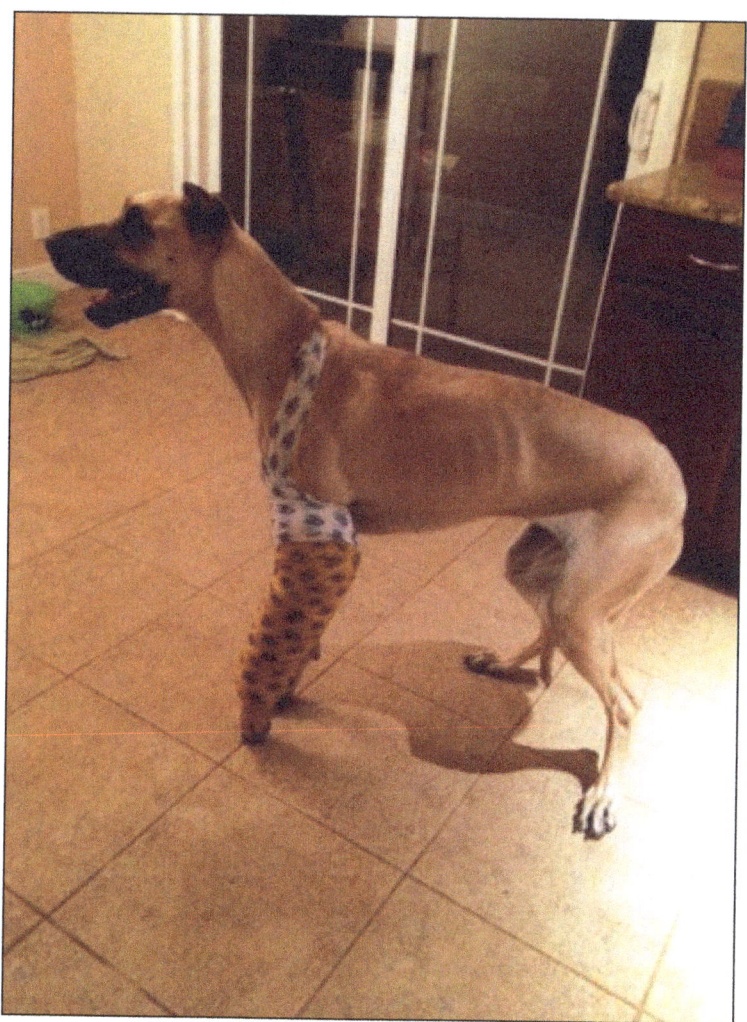

Hannah came to us after being hit by a car on one of the very few traffic circles (roundabout if you are British) in Orange County. Her leg was a mess. A very good orthopedic surgeon put her back together and her leg is now full of pins and plates, but she gets around very well. In fact, it was the same surgeon who helped Delilah (see the story on Delilah) Hannah became very close to Teresa, who by now you know is in love with light colored Danes (in fact all Danes)

Pictures of Hannah after recovery

A miniature pincher wanting to join in the fun.

We took in six male and female miniature pinchers after receiving a call from South Korea. The caller's father lived in California but could not look after the pups. The son asked us if we would get the dogs from the OC shelter as his brother had dropped them there. Teresa went and up all six of them The females were pregnant and two weeks later we had thirteen puppies!

Chapter 59

THE 2020 FIRE NUMBER 1 WHICH STRANDED US APART WITH BEAN SOUP AND NO HOT WATER OR POWER

In late 2020 we had another wildfire. You may have heard that California has lots of wildfires, especially in the forests where political arguments rage about conservation versus logging versus the "natural" cycle of fires which have always served to clean up the brush and dead trees. The situation is complicated because we tend to continue building houses in picturesque areas surrounded by trees, and Southern California is very dry. It is not unusual in Modjeska for us to go six months without rain. My British friends are probably looking out of their windows now at the rain and wondering how often they get a week without any.

One of the frustrations of the fires near Modjeska Canyon is that the big fire of 2007 was not natural, it was started by an arsonist, and the fire of 2020 may have been started by equipment belonging to the electric company (facts still to be confirmed). If they ever caught the arsonist they should make him walk a gauntlet down our canyon, I guarantee he would never make it to the far end.

We heard this new fire was at the far end of Santiago Canyon, about 5 miles from us, and the wind, a vital factor to consider, was gusting to 60 mph but in a direction 90 degrees from us and towards Irvine and Foothill Ranch. As the day progressed, we could see flames on the ridge a few miles away and the smoke was almost horizontal but again blowing away from us. However, the wind can change direction quickly, so we were nervous. Irvine and then Foothill Ranch, both modern housing developments, were mandatorily evacuated, eventually nearly 100,000 people had to leave their homes. During the Monday night we stood outside in the dark in the driveway and watched the flames and the direction of the smoke which was highlighted by the glow behind the hills. The canyons came under voluntary evacuation orders at this point and our power company turned off all power to the canyon, so lights, fridge, freezer, oven etc were all down. We have one cooktop fed by propane and then a few flashlights, you can never have enough flashlights. We only opened the fridge/freezer very briefly hoping to save the food inside and made tea using propane and a pan of water. The wind broke off the trunk of a tree in our yard. This pine tree is probably 50 feet high and it broke at about the 25 foot level falling towards the house but fortunately at an angle so it did not hit the house itself. We cut it up later for firewood but it did not burn very hot, probably as it was so fresh. The wind also stripped all the leaves from the trees and bushes we had carefully nurtured for years to create a visual barrier between the house and the street. This annoyed me intensely of course even in the midst of the fire crisis. Isn't it strange what you can get annoyed about?

In the morning we decided to evacuate the animals. Although the evacuation order was still only voluntary, and the fire was headed away from us, evacuating all of the animals is not a thirty-minute job. A friend and I took 8 dogs to our daughter Rochelle's house in Costa Mesa where they had a large yard to hang in. 3 dogs and the cats went to a Vet office, and the plan was to take the other dogs to another friend, and the farm animals and horses to the County Fair Grounds, as we had been informed that they were taking in evacuated large animals. Teresa called the County to confirm this and they said yes. A neighbor organized a trailer (we don't have one) and the goats, sheep and a pig and the 2 mini-horses were loaded into the trailer. This is not a task to be undertaken lightly, especially the pig which squealed and squealed as it was picked up and loaded. The large Haflinger horse was taken down to a loading point in the canyon where horses were being evacuated.

Well, a little while later, we got a call from the trailer driver. The County Fair Grounds turned us away! This was a surprise and not a pleasant one as we tried to organize evacuation without creating chaos. The driver hauling the trailer wanted to know what he should do so we told him to come back, which he did and unloaded all these animals back into the corral, which is a little easier than loading them up, but still frustrating as the problem of getting the animals out of there was still not solved.

The roads into the canyon were then closed to all except residents, so further attempts to get trailers in to evacuate the farm animals seemed forlorn. The police were making exceptions for some horse trailers but even if we managed to load them again, where were they going to go since our fallback at the Fairgrounds had been closed off. We decided that we would have to stay unless the fire was very close. That's not a popular decision if the evacuation becomes mandatory, but what choice did we have?

At this point we were only able to charge our phones using the car chargers while we sit with the engine on. I don't know about your car charger but mine takes forever. I decided to take my phone, and a battery phone charger borrowed from a friend, and go to another friend's house to get a full charge. I would then return and do the same for Teresa's phone.

This is when the real fun started. I got the phone and battery charged at our friend's house, having gone only about 3 miles from Modjeska, and when I drove back, the police had closed off the canyon and would not let me in! I explained about the animals, my wife, phone charging, food etc, but the answer was "No, and tell your wife to get in her car and leave". They said it might be open in a few hours, so I sat there at the side of the road for four hours. No luck, the answer was still no, and I desperately needed a bathroom. Teresa sounded OK on the phone, but I know now that she was very stressed and feeling very alone, although some neighbors who had also stayed were very supportive. Teresa is a very strong person, but this tested her tremendously. For the two days I was locked out, she managed to eat a can of bean soup heated on the propane stove. I don't know how much wine she drank though!! The police were going house to house in the canyon telling people to leave, but what was Teresa supposed to do with the rest of the animals?

At this point I had retreated to our friend's house where I spent the night on the huge couch and charged the phone again.

We spent much of the next day watching the fire progress. It was still zero % contained and was very close to nearby housing, but fortunately avoiding the canyon. Despite this the police still had the roads blocked. At one point I heard that we could get in at the top of the canyons, which, because the toll road was closed, is about a twenty-mile drive. I drove there and was stopped by the roadblock. One brave driver went round the roadblock and headed into the canyon, but a Sheriff leapt into his car and gave chase. I decided that I didn't want to end up in jail. Apparently, there was another roadblock further in because there was an arson team investigating.

I drove back, thinking I would spend another night at our friend's house. It was about 7pm by this point. I was nearly at the house, and I got a call "I think the road is open!"

It was!

I drove home to a very relieved Teresa and a bottle of cold wine dropped off by a friend with ice, and it was consumed very quickly! While we drank the wine and enjoyed each other's company, we threw away all the food that was in our two fridges and the freezer, as there had been no power and Teresa doesn't like taking chances on that kind of thing. We probably threw away $500 of food.

We still did not have power but we were safe, and together. Planning could now start to get all the animals back, after we drank the rest of wine.

Chapter 60

MOUNTAIN LION

Around the time of 2020 Fire #1, a goat went missing from the corral. We were very puzzled. Over the twenty years we have been here, we have had the occasional escapee, but not a disappearance. I looked up to see if aliens were hovering over Modjeska but could not see anything. A week later, another small goat, Billy who had lived with us for ten years, disappeared. We asked around, posted on Facebook asking if anyone had seen wandering goats or a goat-snatcher but no luck. There were no signs of fence damage.

Then on Thanksgiving morning which always the last Thursday in November for those of you outside the USA, I went to the corral around 7am to feed everyone, and the remaining three goats and Bruce, the sheep we had bottle fed from a baby, were all lying dead in the pasture, legs in the air, one in each corner of the large field. Their throats were slashed, but that was the only apparent damage although I suspect they had been scared half to death. The method of attack is typical of a Mountain Lion, which we do have in our area, but they are rarely seen. Now and again, there is a goat taken somewhere and many years ago someone was killed on a bike trail, but Mountain Lions are solitary creatures. The best theory proposed was that the fire had removed much of their normal prey, small mammals etc, and now they were hungry. Normally the lion will come back over a several days and might carry the kill away. We didn't want the lion back, so we removed the dead goats the same day. That night the lion came back and killed two goats next door. The following week it took a neighbor's llama, and some goats and turkeys elsewhere in the canyons.

We were concerned whether a Mountain Lion would attack our mini-horses, and the general opinion was that this could happen. How do you secure the mini-horses when we do not have a fully enclosed corral? We were told that the lions do not like light and prefer to stay away from humans, so we strung Christmas lights all around the top rail of both corrals, installed solar motion sensor lights in both corrals, and a radio that we left on all night tuned to talk radio. As we were still having power outages whenever it got windy, we borrowed a generator from friends and whenever the power went off, we connected the corral lights, and our fridge, to the generator, so the animals had plenty of light but we in the house were still using flashlights!

The Mountain Lion attacks caused quite a furor in the canyon. Some people thought it was a rogue cat and should be killed and others took the opposite view that basically we were in its territory and should take responsibility for protecting our animals. We had people from the Cougar Conservatory visit and tell us about cougar habits. Apparently, our lights and radio strategy was unlikely to work and full enclosure barns/sheds are the only reliable solution.

A great supporter of the Rescue offered to make our barn "lion-proof" and two great carpenters added a roof extension and impressive sliding barn doors. The barn looked so nice we almost moved in!

The lion attacks continued for some time in the area, as did the controversy about what to do. Sometime later we heard that the lion had been shot. The attacks stopped so it must have been the lion involved.

Chapter 61

2020 FIRE #2

A short while after the Mountain Lion attacks, Teresa woke me up at 12.30 at night. "There's another fire in the canyon, you need to get up". I dragged on some clothes, as I sleep without anything on, and ran downstairs. We were in another power outage because the electric company decided it was windy. Thank you Socal Edison. I had the generator running and the corral above the house on our top driveway looked very festive with its Christmas lights all around the top rail to dissuade the mountain lion from visiting. I had the generator set up only to power the corral lights and the fridge in the kitchen, so we were reliant on flash lights again for personal navigation.

Teresa and I went out onto the main driveway and could see the fire a few miles away towards Silverado Canyon. We learned later that it had started when someone's generator in Silverado Canyon had caught fire and the gasoline had exploded because they had stored it in plastic containers right next to hot generator. Their house was destroyed.

We went out onto the street for a better view and could see that the smoke was heading at 90 degrees to our direction, towards the ocean. There were huge plumes of white and black smoke hundreds of feet into the air set against the black sky and illuminated by the orange glow from the flames, but our air was clear so that was a good sign, for us at least, that the fire was not heading in our direction. We watched for a while and our friend Guy came over. We had stayed at Guy's house during the first fire, and he came over to help if needed, along with his large pick-up truck. Guy also keeps a trailer of man-toys in our wide driveway so if we evacuated that would need to go. Some friends from the deep canyon came up to hang with us as we are on the hill and have a good view of the fire's progress, which you could not see from deeper in the canyon. Our neighbors across the street did not seem to be out yet and that was troubling. They are retired police officers and have animals also, including a German Shepherd that is not the friendliest beast around. Teresa decided she had to make sure they were OK. Braving the unfriendly dog in the enclosed yard, Teresa slipped through the gate and got to the front door alive, waking up our neighbors from a deep sleep. They had not been well and had taken Nyquil to get a good night's rest.

Our little group watched the fire for some time, debating wind direction and whether we would have to evacuate again. We used our flashlights and dragged-out crates from the garage for the dogs and cats and pig, grabbed the box of passports, birth certificates etc. from the office and planned our escape should that become necessary. How to evacuate the two mini-horses at short notice was the big question. Teresa called our neighbor Diane, as they also have a mini-horse, and there was a chance a solution could be found.

About 3.30am, a trailer and truck stopped in the street by our house and a blond lady asked if we needed to move our mini-horses. She had just picked up our neighbor's mini, and had room for ours. We had no idea who she was, or where she was taking them, but neither of those things were important, she was taking them to safety, and we could sort out the rest later.

Fortunately, Surfer, the large Haflinger horse had not returned from the first evacuation yet so we did not have to move him. The family caring for him liked him and were still fostering him.

By this time, we had been outside about 3 hours and the fire were coming much closer, we could see the flames on the far canyon hilltop and were told that Williams Canyon, just over that hilltop, had been hit hard. Police and Fire Department were going up and down the street and around 4pm, police came to the driveway and said, "You need to leave now!"

We explained it was easier said than done with all the animals, but the police response was that we should "Go, now!" Being able to see 50-foot flames around half a mile from the house was also very persuasive.

We managed to load crates of small dogs into the truck of Guy's Australian neighbor Chris who had also come to help. We loaded two loudly squealing pigs, unhappily confined in large dog crates, into the back of Guy's truck, and I loaded cats and other dogs and a suitcase of rapidly grabbed clothes into my Range Rover, the small model, nothing too fancy. For the previous fire I had preplanned and had boxes of family photographs, heirlooms etc, but this time it was a stripped-down evacuation.

That just left seven large dogs, a huge Harlequin Great Dane, two young hyperactive Labradors, an old black Labrador, a fat old yellow Labrador, and two German Shepherds. Imagine if you can, Teresa got all of them in her Honda CRV! It was a little crowded, but I have to say the dogs behaved very well. Unfortunately, I don't have a picture of that. Can you imagine pulling up next to them at the traffic lights?

Before we left the house, I switched off the generator. Some people leave them on to preserve the food in the fridge, but the fire department do not like that at all.

We arrived at Guy's house, about 3 miles away, around 5am. Guy and Theresa have four dogs of their own, all adopted from us. Their dogs were put inside the house while we let 17 of ours out into their back yard which had a nice pool and Jacuzzi and fake turf. The dogs thought this was heaven. One of the pigs went to a different house and Polly, our house pig, went into the three-car garage, which also houses motor bikes and musical equipment as Guy plays drums in a rock band called "The Odds", and we felt pretty "odd" at that moment. For a short while, the two young "hyper" Labradors went into next door's yard where the neighbors were happy to have them, however the labs wanted to be with their buddies and managed to climb on garden furniture to hop the five-foot fence back into Guy's yard. Oh well.

So, how long was this going to last? How would we organize sleeping, feeding, pee breaks etc with our 17 dogs, a pig and their 4 dogs? You may imagine chaos and unhappy canines, but it really was surprisingly calm. There were a couple of dogs-in-the-pool incidents but there was always someone in the yard, so it was funny rather than problematic. Guy's family love dogs and we made the whole thing an adventure.

At night, all the dogs and the pig slept in the garage, where Teresa slept on a blow-up mattress next to a crate for the pig. All the dogs had blankets and beds and settled down calmly because Teresa was there with them, which was the plan. I got the luxury of the couch in the family room and the big screen TV and a beer or two.

This lasted three days. The fire came to within about 300 yards of our house. The Fire department did an amazing job and no houses in Modjeska were damaged, but a number were lost in neighboring Williams and Silverado Canyons.

As I said earlier, one of the consequences of such a fire is a big danger of mud and debris slides when it rains. About 4 months after the fires there was a huge winter rainstorm and some streets and houses in Silverado Canyon and Williams Canyon were many feet deep in mud. This continues to be a danger until the ground cover has regrown. We are lucky that we merely get wet and see water rushing down the steep Grade Rd.

This picture is taken from the gate in our driveway on the night of the second 2020 fire

Before and after pictures from our house looking down into Modjeska canyon

The plane dropping red fire retardant is just over the canyon from us and that house is where Teresa and I got married. This picture is taken from our back corral.

The tree you see in the picture is in our yard about 30 feet from the house and was snapped off at about 20 feet height by the high winds that drove one of the fires

Chapter 62

BYE PACO AND LACEY

In early 2021, Paco and Lacey, the two mini horses which had been with us for eight years, were not doing well. They seemed to be lying down a lot, and not eating as enthusiastically as normal. Animals are like humans, they have good days and bad days, but this seemed to be more than that. They were both approaching thirty years old so we were not totally surprised but were concerned that maybe something more than age was wrong. It started with Lacey, a rather anti-social alpha-female at best, who started to hang at the back of the corral when I was feeding them, rather than dive into the food and shove Paco out of the way if there were any treats going that day, like carrots and apples. For some reason they were both walking slowly and seemingly with difficulty.

We called our friendly farrier, Jesse, who is a neighbor, and asked him to check that their hooves were in good shape and properly trimmed. Jesse is very generous and looks after the Rescue horse's feet for free, although we do sometimes slip him a bottle of Bourbon as a thank you, but don't tell the IRS as they will want 30% of the bottle. Jesse trimmed them both and said they were OK now but there was certainly some deterioration and a check-up from the Horse Vet would be a good idea.

Our Horse Vet, well known to Jesse and all horse people in the area, came to look at Paco and Lacey, but the news was not good. They both had severe laminitis and some other age-related issues which were not treatable. The reluctant advice was that they had both reached their "sell-by" date and should be humanely put down, so they did not suffer any longer. We are always heartbroken when this happens, but we take in a lot of older animals so you can understand that we must go through the process more than we would like.

We arranged for the Vet to come out and do what was necessary and scheduled the livestock removal guy to be there at the same time, 9am. We gave Paco and Lacey special treats the night before and at breakfast lots of carrots and apples and sweet feed. I removed an end piece of the corral fence so the truck could back into the corral. The process took about 45 minutes, but it always seems like hours and hours. Teresa held and stroked Paco while they did Lacey first. I stood a few feet away and couldn't decide whether I wanted to look or not. Once Lacey was down, I wonder if Paco knew what was going on, I hope not.

Then it was over.

Teresa and I went back in the kitchen and held each other and cried. This Rescue thing is not all furry, happy stories.

Then we must get on with life. Teresa was not supposed to be working that day, but someone at her Vet office had not turned up and they had called her to go in and cover, so no more time for weeping, there was work to be done. We had also shut all the dogs in the house, so they did not go crazy while the horse vet was here and visible to them. Of course, some of them had decided to pee all over the living room, so that was my next task. Hot water, bleach and the "towel dance".

Chapter 63

THANK YOU

Thank you for taking a journey with us through some of the days at Modjeska Ranch Rescue over the last 20 years. There were many more days of course and many more stories but I hope I gave you a flavor of this rather crazy life we created. Running a Rescue is equal measures fun, scary, rewarding, exhausting, inspiring and disheartening. We made a difference in over 10,000 animal lives, but the problem of unwanted animals is ongoing and huge. I hope that a few of you might just feel that, if you want to make a difference for something you care about, then you will do it. The world needs more "doers".

Thank you to all of those who have supported us over the years. Not just with money, but old towels, blankets and dog and cat beds dropped in our driveway, events organized for us, help building the corral, transport help, a refuge when we are evacuated, cleaning up around the place and the really essential moral support of those who constantly encourage us with their kind words which we need to stay sane and focused in the face of daily challenges.

Now go and do something today for someone else, for something else, for a cause you believe in. The world needs "Doers". Be a "Doer".

By Russell Taylor

RUSSELL TAYLOR BIOGRAPHY

Russell Taylor was born in Liverpool, England and grew up in Bradford, Yorkshire. He moved to the United States in 1986 to acquire and run companies for a large multinational group. Russell and his wife, Teresa, founded Modjeska Ranch Rescue in 2001. They live in Modjeska Canyon just south of Los Angeles.

Made in the USA
Las Vegas, NV
04 April 2022

46815629R00138